PORTLAND
FOOD

The
CULINARY CAPITAL
of MAINE

Kate McCarty

AMERICAN PALATE

Published by American Palate
A Division of The History Press
Charleston, SC 29403
www.historypress.net

First published 2014

Manufactured in the United States

ISBN 978.1.62619.269.0

Library of Congress CIP data applied for.

CONTENTS

Contents

PREFACE

The most striking part of this project's undertaking is the incredible amount of support I received. I learned that a lot of people within the Portland restaurant and local food industries feel this way about their work too. Everyone I interviewed for this book was so open and generous with their time and thoughts. Portland does indeed feel like a small town but with the best parts of a big city. Never was this more apparent than when I was forced to call up strangers like allegedly grouchy lobstermen and the well-known chefs behind everyone's favorite restaurants. Thank you to those of you who contributed to this project by sharing with me what you are so passionate about.

When I first moved to Portland in 2008, I found the incomparable resource of the Portland Food Map (portlandfoodmap.com), carefully curated by my friend Anestes Fotiades. This site is a staggeringly comprehensive aggregate of news and reviews of every eatery and food-related business in Portland. Thrilled to find myself in a city with so many options, I vowed to print out the map of restaurants, tack it to my wall and eat at every one. Needless to say, that didn't happen, but it did help me explore the culinary diversity of my new city.

At the urging of my friend Elizabeth in Maryland, I created a food blog to share my discovery of Portland's food scene with my family (and my sister gets all the credit for the clever name). In the five years since, I've met a dedicated crew of online turned real-life friends that have been so supportive of my blog. I love that, like me, you never tire of talking about food and that you're always excited about the unusual foods that I dream up. Thank you to all the readers of "The Blueberry Files"; I would have stopped writing a long time ago without your engaging and encouraging words.

Thank you to Greta Rybus, another Portland transport who has found her footing in this town far faster than I did. It was amazing to work with you and to witness your ability to connect with people so quickly. You ask the right questions, laugh in the right places and draw people out so their true selves are revealed to you and your camera. Thank you for your time, your patience and for lending your wonderful eye to this project.

Thank you to the photographers who donated their work, in particular Corey Templeton of Portland Daily Photo, Meredith Perdue, Claire Houston, Anestes Fotiades and Zack Bowen of the Knack Factory. Thank you to my commissioning editor, Katie Orlando, for finding me and thinking that I was well suited for this project. I know that this project took a lot of unseen work on your end, so thank you for believing in me.

I'm grateful for the support of my friends and family; thank you for encouraging me throughout this ambitious project. These words were made possible because my friends make Portland home. Without your company, I wouldn't have fallen in love with Portland and felt the need to share. Thanks in particular go to my mom and my sister for always fielding my frantic stress-related phone calls and for providing endless love and support. My love and gratitude also go to my boyfriend, Andrew, whose confidence in me was unwavering. Thank you for picking up my slack and for always being my dining companion. I look forward to sharing many more meals with you.

Thanks again to those featured in this book and to those who were willing to share their take on the Portland food scene with me. I got such a kick out of hearing, "You know who you should talk to…" and, "If I were writing this book…" I love that I live in a place where everyone has an opinion about food. I wish I had been able to speak with everyone who cooks in Portland, everyone who is passionate about local foods and everyone who cares about our city enough to work toward providing healthy, delicious food for all of us. Instead, I aim to provide you with a snapshot of our culinary scene. It is by no means meant to be comprehensive, as there are new restaurants opening every month and worthwhile work being done every day. I hope you find Portland, Maine, as exciting as I do and, above all, that you find something good to eat here.

Chapter 1

THE EVOLUTION OF SEASIDE DINING

A walk through downtown Portland reveals myriad dining options. The smell of Belgian fries fried in duck fat wafts from the crowded entryway of a small bistro with an orange awning. Across the street, a restaurant's bright-blue exterior and large windows frame a raw bar where customers sip local craft beers and slurp oysters. In the back of a small brick Italian market nearby, thick slabs of Sicilian-style pizza appear quietly on a metal rack. A block away on Fore Street, a small sign and staff loading firewood into an adjacent shed are all that indicate a revered restaurant where inside everything tastes of the sea and nearby farms. Farther down the same street, the finest fish from Maine and Japan is served in a sushi restaurant that rivals any in New York City.

But the city hasn't always had such variety of quality cuisine. Portland was once a largely industrial town, supported by the fishing and lumber industries. A freight train line operated on Commercial Street until the 1980s. The waterfront piers were crowded with warehouses and processing plants, and the harbor's berths were full of fishing and lobster boats. Like many East Coast towns, as these industries faded, the Old Port area became home to more restaurants and shops.

Today, Portland still maintains its working waterfront. A small fleet of lobster boats, seafood processing plants and other marine businesses flanks the water. In fact, a city ordinance gives priority to marine businesses on the piers.[1] But the port is not as bustling with industry as it once was. Instead, it has become a small city with an incredible restaurant scene, supported by tourists and locals alike.

A look up Fore Street in Portland's Old Port shows the varying architectural styles and cobblestone streets that characterize the area. *Photo by Corey Templeton.*

The Sicilian Slab for sale at Micucci's Italian Grocery. In the summer months, slices sell out fast, and there's always a line waiting for the next batch. *Photo by Kate McCarty.*

Thirty years ago, the Old Port wasn't a place many felt safe bringing their family for an afternoon or venturing out to at night. Chef Krista Desjarlais worked in South Portland at the time and remembers that "the Old Port was just starting to shift then. Things were kind of in flux between its days of pirates and being really rundown."[2] She recalls Gritty McDuff's brewpub, which opened in 1988, as one of the first places for people to go and enjoy some corn bread, steamed mussels and good beer.[3] Chef Michael Quigg credited Three Dollar Dewey's, which opened in 1980, with establishing a safe, fun place for people to hang out in the Old Port.[4] Visitors today may find this surprising, as the brewpub model is no longer novel. But in the '80s, these bars were a welcome change from other rough watering holes.

When Fore Street restaurant opened in 1996, Chef Sam Hayward remembers the bars on the other end of his restaurant's street. "We called them 'the Doors of Death'; there were five or six bars on Fore Street that were just nothing but brawling, rowdy, unpleasant places, especially on the weekend. It seemed like there were sirens and police cars going by all the time."[5]

Prior to the revitalization of the Old Port area, restaurants in Portland were scattered throughout the downtown area. Many fondly recall the Village Café, a large Italian restaurant that was located on Newbury Street until 2007. Vincenzo Reali opened the restaurant in 1936 in Portland's Little Italy neighborhood. This family-friendly place was known for its Italian classics like lasagna and veal parmigiana. Reali's grandson, John, eventually sold the restaurant to developers in 2006, and it was demolished to make way for condominiums.[6] The Village Café was one of many popular Italian restaurants in Portland, as were Maria's and the Roma Café. Maria's is still open today and remains the last member of the old Italian guard after the Roma Café closed in 2009.

Now, all that's left of the city's Little Italy neighborhood is Micucci's Grocery and Amato's Deli. Micucci's is full of imported Italian products like olive oil, wine, canned tomatoes and cheese. Bakers in the back of the shop turn out soft, airy half moons of Luna bread and then augment them with sweet tomato sauce and salty mozzarella cheese to make the Sicilian Slab. The grocery and wholesale business is run by the third generation of Micuccis, Rick and Anna, after Rick's parents, Leo and Iris, opened the market in 1949.

Amato's Deli on India Street is known for its Italian sandwiches, which are unlike any other in the country. Founder Giovanni Amato began selling simple meat and cheese sandwiches on his soft white rolls to dockworkers in the early 1900s.[7] These unique sub sandwiches live on through a chain of delis that also

Amato's Italian sandwiches are a Maine specialty. *Photo by Kate McCarty.*

sells pizzas and other Italian classics. The traditional New England split-top bun is carefully layered with American cheese, square slices of ham, peppers, onions, tomatoes, black Greek olives and kosher pickle spears. A sprinkle of salt and pepper and a drizzle of olive oil finish the sandwich.

Several small restaurants existed in the '90s that served American food in comfortable atmospheres. Places like Alberta's Café on Pleasant Street and the Gaslight on Exchange Street inhabited funky spaces and served accessible food. Chef Krista Desjarlais credited Portland's restaurant culture of the '80s and '90s as inspiration for her restaurant, Bresca:

> There were a bunch of places that stuck with me, that made me feel I would go back to Portland because I could afford to rent a little space and just do my thing. Without abiding by the rest of the country and all of the trends, I didn't have to have all of the trappings of fine dining to be successful. It was a much more open, kind of freer environment, like a cheaper San Francisco.[8]

As the Old Port slowly shifted to the retail and restaurant hub it is now, one place in particular is frequently pointed to as the innovator for serving local food and fine dining. Restaurateur Dana Street opened up Street & Co. in 1989 on Wharf Street in the Old Port. The restaurant serves a menu focusing on fresh pasta and grilled seafood from its open kitchen.

Desjarlais recalls the impact the restaurant had on the Portland dining scene: "Street & Co. opened, and that was a huge thing for young cooks. It just felt good inside. I remember going and getting their lobster dish in a paella pan and thinking, 'This tastes so good.' The shift was happening at that point." Street & Co. was the first indicator of where the city's dining culture was headed.

Street & Co. receives frequent praise for advancing Portland's dining culture, but the restaurant could not have succeeded without diners' support. It's also too reductive to portray Portland's restaurant scene as barren before the likes of Street & Co., Fore Street and Hugo's opened. Chef Michael Quigg of Beale Street BBQ views the evolution of the Portland food scene as a continuum. He said, "The beds were laid, the seeds were planted and that's when things started to bloom. Street & Co. was one of the prettiest flowers of that time, but it wasn't the only one and certainly not the gardener."[9] The few restaurants serving good food in Portland helped to cultivate people's appetites for a different type of cuisine.

Chef Hayward sees the caliber of Portland's restaurant scene as an inevitability:

All the elements for Portland's food scene to grow were in place for some time. There was a thriving seafood scene through the '80s. The necessary elements were there, including the farms and artisanal food producers like cheesemakers and brewers and bakers. And when you put all of that together, it was sort of inevitable that it was going to affect the restaurant scene. The foundation of what's going on now was already in place; it just took the right mix of people coming in and an audience that was at least, if not wildly, enthusiastic.[10]

Cities all over the country were experiencing a culinary revolution in the '90s. Chefs shook off corporate, industrial food and started serving fresh, local food from nearby farms. While Portland's restaurant scene had never seen a strong influx of corporate food, diners' enthusiasm for a unique restaurant experience grew. When Sam Hayward and Dana Street opened their restaurant Fore Street in 1996, they stood perfectly positioned to take advantage of this enthusiasm.

Hayward, originally from Ohio, came to Maine in the mid-'70s, looking, he says, to live closer to nature. He ran his own restaurant, 22 Lincoln, in Brunswick before coming to Portland. When opening Fore Street in 1996, Hayward and Street wanted to showcase "local food production, but [involving]…this rustic wood-burning technology."[11]

The evolution of Portland's dining scene continued with Fore Street when Hayward opened the restaurant's doors and began serving wood-roasted meats and seafood. Hayward frequently credits talented Maine food

The modest exterior of Portland's famed Fore Street restaurant. *Photo by Kate McCarty.*

producers for the success of Portland's restaurant scene. But the truth is that Hayward is as instrumental in putting Maine food on the country's radar as any farmer or cheesemaker.

When Fore Street opened, it was immediately successful because of Street and Hayward's reputations, but it had a much smaller menu than it has today. Hayward recalls that diners requested more menu items, eventually expanding to the current two-page menu that changes nightly depending on what's in season. The location of the restaurant was considered outside the Old Port at the time and was surrounded by industrial yards on three sides. Now flanked by a hotel and office buildings, Fore Street restaurant is solidly in the Old Port and in the company of many other fine restaurants.

Desjarlais recalls Fore Street's opening and the impact it had on people's impression of Portland's restaurant scene: "I feel like Fore Street nailed it… with professional service; they care about the product, [and] the plating isn't uptight or forced in any way. The opening of Fore Street sent out the notice that we were more than just lobster places. They shifted us."[12]

Chef Rob Evans says that he always sends people to Fore Street for "the true Maine experience." Of Hayward, Evans says, "He was sourcing things locally before it was trendy. Everyone likes what Sam does there...It's just a really Maine-centric restaurant."[13] Street and Hayward's restaurant is so successful not only because of the fantastic food but also because when you're dining at Fore Street, you feel as though you couldn't be in any other place in the world.

Fore Street has been thriving since it opened in 1996. But it's only within the last ten years that Portland's dining scene overall has taken off. More young chefs are attracted to the area, just as Hayward was in the mid-'70s, for its abundant, quality ingredients. Longtime Portland chefs are taking advantage of the city's national reputation for high-caliber dining by opening second and third restaurants.

Portland is unique with its high concentration of small chef-owned restaurants, like the ones profiled in this book. For every one restaurant and chef mentioned here, there are ten more in Portland equally dedicated or innovative. Together, they create an unexpectedly rich dining scene in a small city in an out-of-the-way state.

Chapter 2
CHANGING TASTES

Sitting in his restaurant, Duckfat, unusually quiet before it opens one morning, Chef Rob Evans laughs when I ask about fine dining in Portland twenty years ago. "There was no high end back then," he says.[14] His former restaurant, Hugo's, was billed as an "Irish bistro" and was run by charismatic Dubliner Johnny Robinson. Evans worked for Robinson in the wintertime, spending the rest of the year in Hawaii. The signature dish at Hugo's Portland Irish Bistro was New England crab cakes, which Evans notes "says it all."[15]

Evans bought Hugo's from Robinson in 2000 and ran the restaurant for thirteen years before selling it to three of his employees. Under Evans's guidance, Hugo's menu slowly changed with the tastes of Portland's diners. Today, Evans sees the story of Hugo's culinary evolution as a microcosm for the city's overall.

Evans is a modest man, describing the restaurants in which he's worked as places rather than names: "Shenandoah Valley" instead of the Inn at Little Washington and "Napa" rather than the French Laundry. He casually credits the Food Network for educating the home cook, and you know his familiarity with the network is because he appeared twice on the cooking competition show *Chopped*. *Food & Wine* magazine named him a "Best New Chef" in 2004,[16] and the James Beard Foundation awarded him "Best Chef: Northeast" in 2009.[17] But the success of his restaurants speaks to Evans's talents in the kitchen even if he will not.

When Evans purchased Hugo's in 2000, his lack of funds forced him to leave the décor unchanged and focus on the food and service. And indeed, that is what Hugo's became known for. The service was impeccable but casual,

Chef Rob Evans (left) with Josh Potocki at a Pocket Brunch event. *Photo by Kate McCarty.*

with servers dressed in jeans achieving the right balance of unobtrusive yet attentive. "We went out of our way to…tone down the pretentiousness of the type of food I did," says Evans. "Dressing our waitstaff in jeans, our bread was biscuits…we always tried to keep the price manageable."[18]

He used his wife's assessments of how his food would be received by the public to temper his self-described "aggressive" style. The approach at Hugo's under Evans was frequently described as "molecular gastronomy"; he prefers to say that his cooking was avant-garde. Whatever you call it, the food was always innovative in taste, texture and presentation.

But innovation is relative, and Evans quickly found that what was popular in California at the French Laundry was too much for Portlanders in 2000. Evans remembers the skepticism of diners: "We opened up with pork belly; I could not sell pork belly. Then we called it 'fresh bacon,' then 'pork breast.' Hard to think of today—I'm waiting for McDonald's to come out with a pork belly sandwich now. It's a good example of what it was like back then; [you] could not push the envelope too much."[19]

Evans began to tweak familiar dishes in order to draw people in while expressing his creativity. He cites his version of cod chowder, a familiar dish though served deconstructed, with cod broth surrounding potato gnocchi and a cod fillet. In the version he served to the *Travel Channel*'s Andrew Zimmern for his *Bizarre Foods* "Maine" episode, the chowder even included cod milt—a fancy word for sperm.[20]

In 2004, Evans was recognized as a "Best New Chef" by *Food & Wine* for his creative use of local ingredients, particularly seafood.[21] After that, he says, he was able to be more aggressive. His 2009 "Best Chef: Northeast" James Beard Award sealed the deal. The restaurant became busier, and people came to expect his signature style.

But despite the success, Evans says the first four years of practiced restraint in the kitchen "clung" to him. "As aggressive as [the menu] was, it was all Maine-based food," he says. "I tried really hard not to bring in Caribbean seafood or tropical fruits. In winter, that became really difficult and boring, but I tried to stick to it. It became a style."[22]

Evans set the stage for his successors with his menu's gradual evolution. In 2013, Evans sold Hugo's to General Manager Arlin Smith and Chefs Andrew Taylor and Mike Wiley. "They're running with the momentum that we had. *Way* more aggressive," Evans says of the restaurant's new iteration.[23] The new owners revamped the restaurant, with dark leather booths, a light wood bar and an open kitchen. Arlin Smith says he sought to defy conventional fine dining rules. "No one has fine dining in this city at a bar, fine dining in a nice booth. It is fine dining, but without all the formalities. We didn't want to conform to anyone's idea of a restaurant," he says.[24]

Hugo's today embodies the transformation of Portland's dining scene. Originally, the chef worried about intimidating customers. Now the new chefs serve dishes like Japanese egg custard *chawan mushi* to enthusiastic diners. Smith credits his former boss for his part in this shift: "It's people like [Rob] who are willing to take those ingredients and knowing that they're not going to be everyone's cup of tea, and it's definitely not your normal restaurant setup, but they still had to give a little bit. And by giving a little bit, it allowed people to slowly come into what Portland was trying to offer."[25]

Today, sitting in his sandwich shop, where the menu is full of simple items without any foams or deconstruction, Evans shakes his head over the difference time has made. "You'd go to Miyake, and you can order pig intestines…place is busy all the time. I'm watching this from '95 up until now, and wow, I can walk off the street and order soy-braised pig intestines. And everyone's on board with this now? I couldn't sell pork belly, but intestines are fine, I guess."[26]

From Irish crab cakes to reimagined American contemporary, the twenty-five years of Hugo's in Portland represents the city's dining identity. It may have taken longer than elsewhere in the country, plus some creative rebranding of today's trendiest ingredients. But Portland's diners are embracing their city's avant-garde interpretation of fine dining with gusto.

Chapter 3

A MAINE STORY ON EVERY PLATE

Support for local products, and in particular food, is strong in Maine. Year-round farmers' markets, local produce in markets and a large number of Community Supported Agriculture (CSA) shares illustrate the demand for local food. One reason for such enthusiasm is an extension of many Portlanders' general love for their state and city. Whether they're from Maine or "from away," people express pride and love for their home or adopted state. Some people are attracted by the ocean's proximity and others the mountains, the surfing, the hiking or the small city living. People speak often about "quality of life" and how it's amazing in Portland.

It's precisely the relative remoteness compared to other parts of the country—Maine isn't exactly on the way to somewhere else in the country—that attracts such loyalists. The state may be slow to adopt national trends, and our industries and economies are smaller than in other states. The state's economic recovery has been predicted to start "next year" for the last three years. Life is a little more precarious on the geographical edges, and Maine is at the end of the line. Efforts in Maine to economize, to be self-reliant and resilient, are noticed and appreciated.

Coupled with a small population, the necessity for independence creates small, accessible communities. If you're interested in making cheese, brewing beer, raising backyard chickens or canning blueberry jam, you can find other people willing to share their experiences with you. Chances are you can talk to the guy who grew the blueberries, the woman who milked the cows or the brewers of Allagash beer. The networks are small, and everyone is willing to share their passion with a fellow enthusiast.

The local foods movement is happening nationwide, and to varying degrees, local foods have always been served in Portland restaurants. Whereas other cities may have lost their regional food systems, Maine has preserved its by necessity. This is not to say that there aren't challenges within the state's farming and local food distribution industries. Many people are working to identify weaknesses and areas of improvement within the existing local foods system.

But unlike other areas of the country, where local farms are pushed hundreds of miles away from a city's center by expanding suburbs, the source of Portland's food is still nearby. "Portland is a provincial town…in the best sense of the word," says Scarborough farmer John Bliss. "It's had that geographic advantage of being close to the province, the countryside, but also the ocean."[27]

Talented chefs are attracted to Portland because of the quality and abundance of local produce, meat and dairy. In turn, the demand for local food grows, attracting more people to farming. But what increasing demand and growth in the local food economy have in common is the community. Some see it as a necessary step in building economic resilience. Others are looking to make choices that favor environmental sustainability. Many believe that serving high-quality food from Maine just makes sense. Whatever the reason, everyone agrees that local food is a worthwhile pursuit.

Chef Sam Hayward, whose restaurant Fore Street is pointed to as the city's premier farm-to-table restaurant, marvels at the emphasis placed on local foods on restaurant menus today. He says, "It's almost inconceivable that a serious restaurant would start up in Maine without at least paying lip service to the local food movement and farm-to-restaurant. It's kind of out of the question."[28]

Every business that serves food in Portland, whether it's a bakery, a diner or a fine dining restaurant, has to make decisions that are right for its business, its customers and its price point. Some local business owners find that local food is more expensive and more work to source but that serving it is in line with their personal values.

Of course, in Maine our selection of local foods is limited by geography— both our northern climate and latitude preclude growing lemons, olive oil or much produce other than root vegetables from December to March. Some chefs and bakers have found that certain products are not available locally or, as unpopular an opinion as it may be, that they do not prefer the local substitution over a higher-quality import.

Blue Spoon serves locally sourced meats and produce, and the focus is always on flavor and hospitality in this cozy East End restaurant. *Photo by Zack Bowen.*

But ultimately, says Portland chef Damian Sansonetti, "If you're not buying some kind of local products from where you are and you're a certain type of restaurant, you're not getting what the whole thing is right now."[29] Sansonetti owns two restaurants in town, the upscale Piccolo, a fine dining Italian restaurant, and the Blue Rooster Food Co., a casual comfort food eatery. Sansonetti sources locally when he finds a superior product but at Piccolo relies on Italian imports like sardines, pine nuts and olive oil.

Sansonetti sources from local farms and markets for produce, seafood, meat and dairy. But he would rather be guided by the quality of ingredients than an adherence to purchasing locally sourced food. Sansonetti recalls working at Bar Boulud in New York and taking a taxicab fifty blocks from the restaurant to the Union Square Greenmarket to purchase local produce. "I ran into this problem in New York," he says. "Is it better to buy something local, or is it better to buy something that's good? There was some stuff that was local, but it was not the same quality as stuff you could get from California or Florida."[30]

Sansonetti noticed that prices rose as locally grown food became more popular, but the quality was unpredictable. In Portland, he says, he purchases directly from the farmers, who are receptive to growing vegetable varieties that Sansonetti otherwise can't find locally. But Sansonetti is wary of chefs using local foods as a marketing trend rather than pursuing high-quality ingredients.[31]

Many chefs struggle with communicating the sources of the food to their customers in an authentic way. Chef Jay Villani serves local food without much fanfare at his three restaurants. Aside from a simple statement on the bottom of the menus noting, "We support local farmers, foragers, and fishermen," the restaurant's sources aren't touted.[32] Villani says, "It's not my job to get that across to the customer. I don't feel like it's my place. I want to believe that's going to come across in what you're eating; you can just taste the difference. If you can taste the difference, that's the first step to understanding…farm-to-table [and] eating locally. You can't force-feed it."[33]

Alison Pray of Standard Baking Co. uses local, organic eggs in her bakery's breads and pastries. "Local, organic eggs are *so* expensive," she says. "But it's so important to me to not eat conventional meat [and] conventional eggs."[34] You wouldn't know from any signage in the shop that the bakery uses as many local and organic ingredients as possible, including flour, fruit, honey, eggs and dairy.

Pray admits to struggling with the marketing of local products, as she doesn't want to bombard her customers with information. But she also recognizes that her customers want to know where their food is coming from, just as she does. "I won't buy food that I don't know where it's come from, but yet, I am reluctant to put big signs out there about it," she says.[35]

At Local Sprouts Cooperative Café, the employees have done just that. A map of Maine is prominently displayed by the counter, with tags labeling the sources of all the food they serve, from sodas to tempeh to tomatoes. Local Sprouts buys from more than forty vendors to serve a menu that is composed of 80 percent local foods. Member-owners Abby Huckel and Kelly Rioux say that serving mostly local foods is more work and, at times, limiting. Rioux says, "We work with a lot of local vendors who are amazing…" "But sometimes the kale freezes," adds Huckel, "and that's just the reality of this

Above: Jay Villani's restaurant Local 188 started as a small, artsy tapas bar and is known for its Spanish cuisine, creative cocktails and comfortable atmosphere. *Photo by Kate McCarty.*

Left: Baguette dough at Standard Baking Co. rising before baking. Standard is known for its European-style breads and pastries. *Photo by Kate McCarty.*

Portland has many chef-owned restaurants serving locally produced meats and produce like this hanger steak served at Blue Spoon. *Photo by Zack Bowen.*

Guinea hogs at Miyake's Freeport farm are being raised for their flavorful meat. *Photo by Kate McCarty.*

business."[36] Rioux says that sourcing locally is not only more work but frequently more expensive as well: "Many restaurants here are doing a lot of local stuff, but they might also be supplementing the rest of their menu with stuff that's a lot cheaper in other areas."[37]

But both Rioux and Huckel believe in working for a business that is in line with their personal values, so they don't mind the extra work. They both believe that the challenges of sourcing local foods are opportunities to change the system that makes local food inaccessible. Rioux says, "We have priorities and values that we try to meet with all of our products. And if we're not, then we want to have a conversation about it. We want to educate people about their food system and why this is really hard, so more businesses use more [local] ingredients."[38]

Chef Masa Miyake and his business partner, Will Garfield, are looking for more local and sustainable sources for the food they serve in their three Japanese restaurants. The menu focuses heavily on seafood, and Miyake was sourcing the Japanese and European fish that he was used to in his native Japan. But after Miyake and Garfield took a trip to northern Japan together, they realized the region's similarities to Maine.

Garfield says, "Masa drew the parallels between where he grew up in Japan—as far as climate, access to the ocean and ingredients—and Maine. The seasons are very similar; what you're using during certain times is very similar. So that's our new focus, offering Japanese food with a Maine spin on it." Miyake began sourcing local mackerel instead of Spanish mackerel, local monkfish liver and northern New England whelk.[39]

Miyake sources many of his ingredients from local farmers and seafood companies and even started farming his own produce and raising pigs. He is raising and breeding three types of pigs at his house in Freeport, including the rare Mangalitsa breed, which is frequently referred to as the "Kobe beef of pork." Three litters of pigs were born on the farm this spring, some of which are a unique hybrid of two heritage breeds. Neighboring Wolfe's Neck Farm in Freeport is raising twenty feeder Guinea hogs that are destined for the menu at Pai Men Miyake. The pork is served at the popular noodle bar in ramen and dumplings.[40]

In switching to a menu that he describes as "sustainable Maine," Garfield says, "Those are some of the things over the years we're trying to get more in sync, [to] find our own producers for. With the farm, we wanted to offer a way for our customers know where our product is coming from."[41] In doing so, Garfield and Miyake have created a unique dining experience in Portland by offering traditional Japanese food made with local ingredients.

In an extreme example of farm-to-table dining, one chef set up his restaurant literally on the farm. The Well at Jordan's Farm is the summertime project of chef and owner Jason Williams. The restaurant is not much more than a small mobile kitchen that sits next to the farm stand. Surrounded by picnic tables, gazebos and the pick-your-own flower fields, Williams serves dinner three nights a week in the summer months, designing that evening's menu using the farm's produce after a walk-through of the farm stand to see what's available.

The chalkboard menu, BYOB policy and counter service belie the quality of food served at the Well. Seared hake served with roasted new potatoes, braised radishes and baby spinach with lemon-butter sauce was a popular dish on the menu last summer. Using fresh, seasonal ingredients and a light hand in the kitchen, Williams serves simple, quality food in a relaxed environment.

A Culinary Institute of America graduate, Williams most recently worked in the kitchen of Portland's Back Bay Grill, one of the city's few white-linen, fine dining restaurants, under Chef Larry Matthews. When it was time to move on from the Back Bay Grill, Williams wanted a way to continue to support Jordan's Farm. Williams says:

> I just really love being here on the farm. I'm trying to showcase what Jordan's has to offer, maybe in a different way than [people] are familiar. Jordan's has been around forever; they have a strong clientele. This was more to show people what else they can do with the same stuff. Braised radishes, for example. People say, "Oh, I've never had cooked radishes!"[42]

In addition to produce from Jordan's Farm, Williams buys from other Cape Elizabeth farms like Green Spark Farm and Alewive's Farm. He sources his seafood from Portland's Browne Trading Company; organic, pasture-raised chicken from Serendipity Acres in North Yarmouth; and grass-fed beef and veal from Harris Farm in Dayton.[43] Williams even manages to serve all local produce and protein at reasonably priced rates for a fine dining restaurant.

Rather than take advantage of Cape Elizabeth's reputation for well-off restaurant clients, Williams chose to list a suggested price for each menu item. He also wanted to continue the tradition of farm stands' honor system for payment. He says his pricing system keeps his cooking honest:

> I wanted people to be like, "Twenty-three dollars for chicken!? I'm only putting in twenty!" but then sit down and eat it and be like, "Okay, that

The Well at Jordan's Farm is a seasonal restaurant serving fresh, local meals using produce from Jordan's Farm. *Photo by Meredith Perdue.*

was worth twenty-three dollars," and then come back. Those are the moments that keep me pushing on every plate. Thinking they could put in ten dollars here, but I want them to realize what it's worth and be happy with what they paid.[44]

The day I visit Williams, he is prepping for a wine dinner the following night. He works alone in his small kitchen, not much larger than a garden shed. It's a rainy, late summer afternoon, and Williams comments how beautiful the farm is this time of year. You might think that such a restaurant borders on satire of the local food movement. But when you listen to Williams speak about his motivations for starting the restaurant and for serving the food he does, you realize that he's nothing but earnest. "I wanted to have a nice place where people could eat good food," he says.[45]

Williams is a young chef, quick to laugh, and has structured his life so he can pursue his other passion in the wintertime. He's an avid snowboarder and travels with the Burton snowboard team as its private chef. When asked if he enjoys riding in Maine, he diplomatically replies, "I've been spoiled; there's other places I would go, if I had to pick."[46] East Coast snowboarding might be the only thing about which Williams is a touch elitist.

While it is hard to generalize the attitudes surrounding local foods in restaurants, one thing is for certain: people are proud to call Portland, Maine, home and are dedicated to supporting local businesses. The degree to which that translates to local foods in restaurants varies, but with so many options for dining in Portland, everyone, including the most strident locavore, is sure to find a meal that makes them happy.

Chapter 4

RESTAURANT FAMILIES

Few chain restaurants exist in downtown Portland—a handful of Dunkin' Donuts, several Starbucks shops and a few national hamburger franchises operate in the Old Port. The fast-food chains are sequestered in the outskirts of the peninsula by the onramp to the highway and the area surrounding the Maine Mall in South Portland. The city flirted with banning "formula businesses" on the peninsula in 2006, but the zoning was repealed following protests from the business community.[47] For the most part, Portland restaurants are owned by chefs. For some chefs, the success of an initial restaurant has prompted a second, a third and, in one case, a fourth.

Year after year, the question of a restaurant "bubble" arises, and to date, said bubble continues to inflate. More people visit Portland every year and continue to fill the city's restaurants. Issues like available restaurant space and seasonality are of increasing concern, but many chefs continue their quest for second locations. Some say that they're satisfying a fundamental need, while others express a desire to provide promotions for their talented staff. The reasons behind multiple restaurant openings are as varied as the menus they serve.

Arlin Smith, general manager of Eventide Oyster Co. and Hugo's, came to own his first restaurant after working in it for four years. Sitting in a posh leather booth on an unseasonably hot September afternoon, Smith remembers his first impressions of Portland and Hugo's. "This restaurant itself was the reason Roxanne and I moved up here," he says. "We had a tasting menu here in the middle of winter, and within a month, we moved up here. If this town can support this type of food and service, we want to be a part of it in some way. And now in a bigger way, since we purchased it."[48]

Smith started working in the front of the house at Hugo's (with his partner, Roxanne Dragon, at the bar). When neighboring business Rabelais Books moved south to Biddeford, Smith and two co-workers leased the space to open Eventide Oyster Co. While not his dream restaurant, Smith knew that a New England–style raw bar would be successful in Portland:

> *We felt responsibility to the city…We were like, "What does Portland need?" And all of us were like, "It's got to be an oyster bar." [But] what can we do different? What can we do that's really traditional that people don't even see because we're so used to the commercialization of New England? The thick chowders that are just like paste…people think that's what a real chowder is.*[49]

Instead, Eventide serves a clam chowder that is light yet intensely flavorful, with tender (never chewy!) clams. Eventide is wildly popular, so Smith and his partners were right that Portlanders would embrace their vision of a raw bar.

Not long after Eventide's opening, they were presented with the opportunity to purchase Hugo's from longtime chef and owner Rob Evans. The three men had already been running the restaurant under Evans for a few years. And just like Evans, they had another successful restaurant to help fund their dreams. Smith points out that a crowd-pleasing restaurant can pave the way for a more esoteric one. "I think the multiple thing is what allows the small restaurants to survive. Rob [has] Hugo's, and then they open up their cash cow, Duckfat. That gives you the stability to take chances and flourish."[50] The same can be said of Smith's two restaurants. The steady income from Eventide gives them more freedom on the menu at Hugo's.

The varied concepts at some chefs' multiple locations indicate their culinary creativity. Chef Harding Lee Smith owns four "rooms": a steakhouse, an Italian corner eatery, a waterfront seafood restaurant and a casual American tavern. All four locations serve accessible food and bear Smith's signature restaurant style. Steve and Michelle Corry ran the successful Five Fifty-Five for years before going in a different direction with their French bistro Petite Jacqueline. The three disparate restaurants in Chef Jay Villani's restaurant group serve Spanish tapas, Latin American cuisine and southern-style barbecue. Chef Damian Sansonetti appeals to different palates with the high-quality "low-brow" food at Blue Rooster Food Co. and the simple, quality southern Italian cuisine he serves at Piccolo.

Eventide Oyster Co. is a popular New England–style raw bar from the owners of Hugo's. *Photo by Kate McCarty.*

David Turin—the chef behind David's, David's 388 and David's KPT—has opened twelve restaurants in his lifetime. David's on Monument Square has been in business for sixteen years. In what was to be his final project, Opus 10 is Turin's eighteen-seat restaurant that serves a prix fixe menu with one seating per night. While the menu changes regularly, Turin has featured small courses of scallops with figs, butter-poached lobster with a vanilla bean *buerre monté* and half a quail with a foie gras medallion.

When his search for desirable real estate in Portland failed, Turin decided to open the restaurant inside his existing space at David's on Monument Square. He renovated the back of the restaurant to create a private dining room with a small kitchen. The minute restaurant-within-a-restaurant has been well received, although Turin wishes more people would visit Opus 10. "There's like a million reasons why this is a really bad business plan," he says. "So if we were doing it for the money…why would we do that? We're doing it because it's the food I wanted to cook—it's the restaurant I really always wanted to do."[51]

As we talk, Chef Turin repeatedly mentions the business of running a restaurant. After thirty years in the industry, with four restaurants and hundreds of employees, it's impossible to ignore. Part of the reason Turin says he has continued to open restaurants in Portland is to provide continued employment for his staff:

Invariably you take a restaurant the size of Hugo's or David's 388 or [David's on Monument Square], *and there's only so much revenue. And so…the people working for get you get to a point where they're stifled. Actually…my single biggest driver of opening new restaurants is because I have these people* [who are] *literally like family. They're developing talent, and there's nowhere for them to go because the restaurant's only so big. So we'll open something else.*[52]

But Turin eventually talks himself around to a different motivation for growing his restaurant group. He has internalized the ubiquitous "what do you want to be when you grow up" question from his childhood. As a result, he says, "I equate this whole sense of what you are…has everything to do with what you do. It's just in my DNA. I'm a chef/restaurateur. If I'm not opening restaurants, who the hell am I? You asked me earlier, 'Why did you continue to open all these restaurants?' Part of it could just be obsession, part of it existential."[53] Chefs are often single-minded because of the all-consuming nature of their work. Coupled with the energy level required to run a business, successful chefs frequently find themselves pursuing other restaurant projects.

Will Garfield of the Miyake Restaurant Group is twenty-five years old and a Cape Elizabeth native. He describes his business partner, Chef Masa Miyake, who is from Japan's Aomori Prefecture, as indefatigable: "He's almost fifty-three now, and he has comparable, if not more, energy to myself as far as attacking stuff on a daily basis and never…closing his eyes for a shortcut."[54]

Together, Garfield and Miyake have opened three restaurants in Portland in the last five years. Their most recent project, the Miyake Diner, is a reimagining of their original sushi bar's location. The first restaurant, dubbed Food Factory Miyake, grew in popularity until Garfield and Miyake leased a much larger space on Fore Street. Garfield describes the new Miyake space as "more of an oasis, much quieter," compared to the old location on Spring Street. "We were trying to elevate ourselves to compete with Five Fifty-Five, Fore Street…to tap into a clientele we didn't have before."[55]

In 2010, Garfield and Miyake opened Pai Men Miyake, serving ramen, sushi rolls and small plates, including pork belly buns. Despite a strong following at the Miyake Spring Street location, Garfield remembers the struggle of opening their second restaurant: "[It] was a long battle for us, as far as educating the public, in that ramen is not the sixty-nine-cent stuff you find at Hannaford."[56] Fortunately, everyone came onboard, and now Pai Men Miyake is full of diners slurping noodles behind its steamy windows.

The third Miyake location is an *izakaya*-style diner with traditional cooked Japanese dishes and a full sake bar. The Spring Street location has been remodeled since its days of Food Factory Miyake, Garfield remembers, "with the Pepsi fridge in the back in plain view and a few broken Ikea chairs."[57] After it failed to catch on at Pai Men Miyake, Garfield is determined to bring an extensive sake selection to Portland in his newest restaurant.

With the opening of this third restaurant, Garfield says that he and Miyake are done opening restaurants in Portland. They'll focus on ensuring good food and good service in all of their establishments. Any expansion will be on the restaurant group's farm. Chef Miyake's unbounded energy might possibly generate beer and sake brewing projects in the future.[58]

But with three restaurants to run, Garfield isn't thinking too much ahead. The rapid expansion of his restaurant group has him busy enough. "I don't know when the tipping point will be; I've been saying it's coming for two years now," he says. "But we'll see. Portland's a good place to have a restaurant right now, and I've loved seeing it progress."[59]

Looking ahead to the numerous restaurants in the works, many people, chefs and business owners wonder how many places visitors and locals can continue to support. With Portland receiving increasing attention from the rest of the country, more and more people are coming to visit for our high-quality food and dining scene. Some, like David Turin, think that that very attention might turn out to be a mixed blessing: "I'm a little scared about the Portland food scene, because I think that with the publicity we've gotten, more corporate investors will jump in and change the dynamic."[60]

This national attention coupled with new hotel construction and the high cost of large restaurant renovations may very well influence the source of the money behind new restaurant projects. The impact of our restaurant industry's recent growth remains to be seen. But even the largest local restaurant "empire" in Portland doesn't compare to a corporate restaurant group. Multiple restaurants from our favorite chefs show the talent, ingenuity and creativity of Portland's culinary professionals.

Chapter 5

THE INFLUENCE OF CHEFS "FROM AWAY"

Chef Damian Sansonetti may have moved to Maine to settle down, but he still keeps a New York City pace. In the two years since he's relocated from Queens to Portland, he has thrown five pop-up dinners and opened two restaurants, and his wife had a baby. On the day I meet him, we talk for an hour, and then, with a big smile, he says he's "in the weeds," prepping for New Year's Eve dinner service the next night.[61] Five years as the executive chef at the perpetually busy Bar Boulud must have taught him some time-management skills.

Diners have praised Sansonetti's new restaurant Piccolo (named for both the diminutive space it occupies and his newborn daughter) since its opening in November 2013. He runs the kitchen with his wife, Ilma Lopez, who also worked for Daniel Boulud, as well as Ferran Adrià. By their mid-thirties, both chefs had accomplished careers and were looking for something new. The couple visited Portland for a weekend at the urging of Rod Mitchell of Browne Trading Company. In one day, Sansonetti and Lopez ate at four restaurants: the Lobster Shack at Two Lights, Bresca, Duckfat and Fore Street.

Impressed by the quality of the restaurants in Portland, the two considered Portland as their next move. They saw Portland as an attractive place to open a restaurant rather than continue on their path of running high-end restaurants in New York. Sansonetti says, "We had reached…pinnacles in our careers for certain things. We just wanted another side of life."[62]

Lopez moved first while Sansonetti began the slow process of replacing himself at Bar Boulud. Lopez became the pastry chef at Grace in Portland.

She turned out meticulously constructed desserts using foams, gelées and meringues in the church turned restaurant. After her maternity leave, Lopez joined Sansonetti in the kitchen of Piccolo, where the two cook together nightly. Chef Rob Evans of Duckfat describes Sansonetti as "some of the best talent in town right now."[63]

At Piccolo, Sansonetti serves what he describes as "rustic yet refined" food in the twenty-seat restaurant. His cooking is in the tradition of southern Italian cuisine, which is more Mediterranean than "Mamma Mia." Sansonetti enthusiastically describes a dish he served at his Sunday Supper series, a special prix fixe menu served only at the six seats at Piccolo's bar:

> *I got in a whole collar from a local swordfish, and they're called "butterball" this time of year because they're so fatty. I braised it in charred tomatoes, olives, olive oil and oregano. Then I took all that meat off, and it was so tender. We put it on a huge cutting board that I had and plated it up with some broccoli rabe, some of the olives, tomatoes…and when we gave it to them, there was that excitement, that sense of "wow."*[64]

Sansonetti and Lopez are part of a wave of young chefs moving to Portland "from away," the colloquial term locals use to describe anywhere outside Maine. Chefs are increasingly attracted to the area for the caliber of the restaurant scene coupled with relatively inexpensive rents. Chefs are also drawn to Portland for the access to great ingredients, the supportive culinary community and the overall low cost of doing business.

Sansonetti says they looked at several spaces before finding the space for Piccolo. "All the other restaurants that are opening up, we've looked at all of those spaces. And each one had its own little challenge to it where we [didn't] want to invest that much time and/or money into that spot. Or it didn't fit the concept we wanted right away."[65] His new restaurant is in the space that housed Krista Desjarlais' restaurant, Bresca, for seven years. While only a few months elapsed between restaurants, some renovations were still needed. Sansonetti did some building upgrades and spruced up the interior.

Chef David Turin recalls a conversation with a New York City chef in which she revealed that her restaurant's monthly rent was more than what Turin pays in a year to lease his Monument Square restaurant space. Turin says that this takes some pressure off chefs and allows them to approach their businesses in a different way. "It's so inexpensive, in terms of rents, that you can afford to run a little restaurant where the food matters more than the bottom line," he says.[66]

Chefs Damian Sansonetti and Ilma Lopez moved to Portland from New York to open Piccolo, a fine dining Italian restaurant. *Photo by Zack Bowen.*

But New York chefs used to the year-round crowds in their restaurants will find a distinctly different pace in Portland. While not as seasonal as some Maine tourist towns, Portland is decidedly quieter in the wintertime. Chef Krista Desjarlais says that it's a bit nerve-wracking as a small business owner in a seasonal town. She says, "You can take a walk around town on any midweek [winter] evening, and we're all at the window waving at you, 'Hey, c'mon in!' It's all relative when it comes to paying the bills."[67]

The recent boom in restaurant openings has led to less available restaurant space in Portland. The relative scarcity has created more ambitious renovations, like the cavernous In'finiti Fermentation & Distillation and the multistoried Boone's Fish House & Oyster Room. Finding a restaurant in relative turnkey shape like Piccolo is becoming a rarity. The expense of a space's upgrades may eventually outweigh the benefits of Portland's inexpensive rents.[68]

Portland has come a long way in its connection to the food culture of other cities, particularly New York. Chef Rob Evans recalls an incident that illustrates local diners' increasing connectivity: "I cooked with Daniel [Boulud] at Hugo's in 2004. I called up *Portland Press Herald* to tell them Danny Boulud was coming…and they asked who she was." Today, though, Evans says of Portlanders, "They're still savvy; they're not ignorant. They're not going to go spend a lot of money at a restaurant and keep going back just because it's hip or following some trend."[69]

Sansonetti, for his part, isn't looking to rest on his laurels. "I think people expect a little something from us in certain ways," he says. "And we don't want to disappoint them and then surprise them at times too." Sansonetti's accomplished background and dedication to hospitality make him a welcome addition to the Portland dining scene.

As the Portland restaurant industry grows, and as it receives more attention from national press outlets and chefs "from away," it will, of course, change. But some believe that what makes our city so attractive as a dining destination is what makes it the most vulnerable. As the restaurant market grows, it becomes more attractive to larger brands or investors rather than small, chef-owned restaurants. And with the presence of larger restaurants or chains, many fear a loss of the character on which the city prides itself.

Portlanders are proud that their city attracts big-name talent like Sansonetti and Lopez. Many talented chefs from Maine and from away chose to open their restaurants in Portland because of strong support for local foods, the number of small restaurants and great access to local products. But as the restaurant industry grows, concerns about the sustainability of that growth arise. Smart business development practices are needed to preserve what locals and tourists alike love about Portland's dining scene.

Chapter 6

PRESERVING FARMS IN VACATIONLAND

Between the cold weather, the snow and the rocky soils, you'd be forgiven for thinking that farming in Maine is difficult. And it's true that, unlike in the Midwest, where rich, loamy topsoil stretches on for miles, southern Maine has a considerable amount of wetlands and ledge that isn't suitable for farming. But with plentiful sunlight, abundant water and rich soil, Maine supports a strong, diverse agriculture industry. Many of these farms are located in the more populated areas of southern Maine, close to Portland, where the growing conditions are milder and the demand for locally grown food is high. While Portland has the largest population of any Maine city, it only occupies fifty-two square miles and is in proximity to farmland that hasn't been lost to sprawling development.

Maine farmers face unexpected challenges. Some farmers can't grow enough to meet ever-increasing demand. Others just starting out or looking to expand convey how difficult it is to find and afford farmland. Despite these hurdles, all continue to farm because of the support of a community that appreciates local food and farmers.

Penny Jordan is the fourth generation to farm the family's land and sees strong support for locally grown food from her community. "The demand is huge. I now have to say to people who want to become wholesale buyers, 'I'm sorry, I am maxed with wholesale. I can't grow enough,'" she says.[70] Other area farmers echo Jordan's sentiments, as they increase production to meet a growing demand.

Jordan's Farm in Cape Elizabeth, six miles south of Portland, is a diversified vegetable farm that sells local products ten months out of the

A rainbow of radishes at the Portland Farmers' Market. *Photo by Phil Jellen.*

year. The farm is a relatively large one for southern Maine, with sixty to seventy acres cultivated annually, but small compared to a Maine potato farm in northern Maine, where the average size of a farm is three hundred acres.[71] "I tell all my friends who are [potato] farmers in Aroostook County that we're a garden; they're farmers," laughs Jordan.[72]

Jordan's retail farm stand is nestled between the towering old farmhouse, greenhouses and farm fields rolling down to meet the Spurwink River marshes. The stand sells fresh produce, meat, cheese and value-added products. The community shows its support for the farm, buzzing around the stand on a summer afternoon. Locals peruse bins of tomatoes, eggplants, beets, greens and even a refrigerator of local meats, cheeses and wine. The parking lot is filled with a constant stream of cars. Customers chat with the farmworkers as they wash, sort and package produce in the back of the stand. It's these consumers, who believe in supporting their community's local food, who continue to make the success of a diversified vegetable farm in southern Maine possible. And Jordan knows it. "We're blessed to be in Cape Elizabeth, where we have a highly educated consumer base," she says. "They know that if they participate in agriculture, then the farm will be here."[73]

In an effort to maintain the rural and agricultural character of the area, Jordan is a member of the Cape Farm Alliance, a network of local farmers and producers that promotes local food while working to preserve the community's farmland.[74] Applying the mantra of longtime Maine Organic Farmers and Gardeners Association (MOFGA) executive director Russell Libby, who was a key figure in promoting Maine's local, organic agriculture, the Cape Farm Alliance works to convey the message that if town residents spend only a few dollars a week at local farms, the net effect is millions of dollars per year.[75] The community's support of local farms is critical, particularly for Cape Elizabeth, where high property values can lure landowners into selling their land to developers. "Cape Elizabeth is known for houses, not farms," says Jordan.[76]

Cape Elizabeth has the highest income per capita in the Greater Portland area, and many wealthy New Englanders' large second homes perch on the rocky shoreline overlooking the ocean.[77] It's home to Portland Head Light, one of Maine's most iconic lighthouses, and the Lobster Shack at Two Lights, where thousands of visitors a year make the pilgrimage to eat a lobster roll on picnic tables that frequently receive ocean spray from waves crashing onto granite slabs nearby.

But Cape Elizabeth is neither solely a tourist attraction nor a playground to the rich. Just over nine thousand people call the area home and are attracted to the quality of life that Cape offers. The surrounding farmlands, the rural character and the coastal feel all contribute to a quality of life that residents value. As property values rise, it's tempting for landowners to make the profitable choice to sell their land for real estate development. Fortunately, town planners and nonprofit organizations are working together to keep farming a viable option in the area.

In 2004, looking for a way to raise capital for the business, the Jordans placed 47 acres of undeveloped farmland into a conservation easement.[78] This voluntary agreement between the Cape Elizabeth Land Trust and Jordan's Farm makes the land unavailable for anything other than farming. In return, the business benefits from a tax deduction and lower property taxes. Jordan is also ensuring that the land surrounding her farm, which also borders a 493-acre tract of the Rachel Carson National Wildlife Refuge, will always be farmed rather than parceled off for development.[79]

Jordan knows that her customers value her family's farm for more than fresh vegetables at dinnertime: "The fact that we are present here in the center of multiple developments…it's not about us selling food that impacts [people's] lives; it's about us growing food and keeping this open space and keeping that picture of where food comes from. They see it when they pass every day, and I think that impacts people's lives."[80]

Penny Jordan is the fourth generation to farm her family's property. She sells her produce to Portland restaurants and markets, as well as on the farm. *Photo by Greta Rybus.*

Austin Chadd of Green Spark Farm and his display of rare and heirloom vegetables at the Portland Farmers' Market. *Photo by Kate McCarty.*

A fixture in the farming community, Penny Jordan is a good person to know if you're looking to farm. Austin and Mary Ellen Chadd of Green Spark Farm found their fifteen-acre parcel of farmland in Cape Elizabeth through Jordan's connections. After completing MOFGA's Journeyperson farm training program, a two-year course designed to "fill the continuing education gap between apprentice and independent farmer,"[81] the Chadds moved from a smaller, leased parcel to the land they farm now.

Mary Ellen and Austin came to Maine after studying ecological agriculture in college and working on farms in New York, Washington and Latin America.[82] They represent a trend in Maine farmers: younger people who chose farming as an occupation rather than generational farmers.

Andrew Marshall, MOFGA's Educational Programs director, has seen an increase of new farmers in Maine through the trainings he offers. "We've really seen there was a big pulse during the economic downturn, people re-strategizing their priorities and careers. 2007 to 2010 was when we really saw steep growth, which has slowed down since, but it's been growing pretty consistently."[83]

MOFGA's Journeyperson program trains 25 people per year, and 250 people have completed the program since its inception in 1999. Resources like these make Maine an attractive place to farm and serve as a model for other New England states that have also implemented similar training programs for new farmers.

At Green Spark Farm, Mary Ellen and Austin Chadd use the marketing skills they gained in their apprenticeship and the Journeyperson program to distinguish their farm's products. Growing rare and heirloom vegetable varieties like Romanesco cauliflower, totsoi and Shishito peppers, the Chadds work year round in unheated greenhouses and attend Portland's winter and summer farmers' markets.

After three years on their current land, Mary Ellen and Austin have a 140-member Community Supported Agriculture (CSA) program and sell to Portland restaurants Hugo's, Eventide Oyster Co. and Miyake and the Small Axe food truck. But in a sentiment echoed by many Maine producers, Austin points to the difficulty of land access: "The biggest challenge is finding that medium between having your own land that's affordable and being near markets. The biggest reason we haven't packed up and moved to a more rural place where we can afford our own land is that we have such an amazing market here."[84]

In neighboring Scarborough, the local land trust worked to connect farmers looking to grow their business with the land that is now Broadturn Farm. After farming for three years in Cape Elizabeth, farmers John Bliss and Stacy Brenner found Scarborough Land Trust in the process of preserving 430 acres of land that was a family farm for nearly 150 years.[85]

With money provided by local, state and federal fundraising, the Scarborough Land Trust purchased the land and began searching for interested farmers. Partnering with neighboring Snell Family Farm, Bliss and Brenner successfully applied and now cultivate fifteen acres of organic vegetables and flowers.

The arrangement between Broadturn Farm and Scarborough Land Trust includes a conservation easement with development restrictions and a thirty-year lease ensuring that both parties' interests are satisfied. The farmers can invest in the property as a business by making improvements to irrigation, drainage and existing buildings, and the land trust sees a large parcel of farmland preserved.[86]

Through this process, Bliss became a huge advocate for land trusts and their work to preserve farmland and the rural character of an area. He says:

If it's a nonprofit that owns the property, the landlord is not emotionally connected to the place the way an individual would be. I feel so lucky that we don't have this family dynamic, which really is a huge hurdle for a lot of farms. I'd say 50 percent of the time, that transition between the old generation and the new generation is the demise of the farm. They can't agree, and they move somewhere else; no other people in the family are willing to take it over, and it gets sold. And most of the time, it gets sold for development.[87]

According to Maine Farmland Trust, one-third of Maine's farmland will be in transition in the next five years due to aging farmers.[88] With plenty of farmland available and an increasing number of interested young farmers looking to farm in Maine, the work of state and local land trusts has never been more important.

Bliss theorizes that Maine stands to learn valuable lessons about land preservation and development from neighboring states. He cites an oft-referenced belief that Maine moves at a slower speed than the rest of New England. National trends tend to arrive a few years later in Portland, which then means that there's plenty of time for people to see any undesirable consequences play out first. Bliss says:

In terms of development, the land conservation movement has not had enough time to get up and get organized before sprawl came into Connecticut. Southern Maine has had that chance; there's been fair warning. Mainers talk about Massachusetts in really negative tones, and what they're talking about is the traffic and the lack of community, all these things brought on by urban and suburban development. Because we're on the edge of civilization up here in Maine, we've had the time to absorb these lessons and prepare for it.[89]

Neither Bliss nor Brenner is from Maine, both having moved here precisely for the quality of life that southern Maine offers. Now they feel fortunate to be pursuing their love of farming on a property that protects and contributes to what they love about living in Maine.

The challenge of preserving farmland is a significant one, what with the amount of work required to connect farmers and available farmland. But eating locally has never been just a trend in Maine. Support for the farms that feed Portland will continue to grow and help to preserve these resources.

Chapter 7

THE ALCHEMY OF CHEESEMAKING

W hen asked if he ever gets bored while heating cheese curds and whey, a slow process that requires constant stirring for upward of an hour, cheesemaker Tyler Renaud replies seriously, "We put the 'chi' in 'cheese.'" I laugh, and he says, "I've been waiting eight months to use that joke."[90] Apparently, Renaud and Head Cheesemaker Dorothee Grimm have plenty of time to think while carefully preparing Silvery Moon Creamery's cheeses at Smiling Hill Farm.

Cheesemaking is a gradual and precise process; milk must be heated slowly, bacterial cultures added at just the right temperature, curds drained thoroughly and fresh cheeses aged in exact conditions to encourage beneficial molds and prevent spoilage. On the day I visit, Renaud and Grimm are working on turning 160 gallons of cow's milk into 140 pounds of cheddar cheese curds. They will then package the curds up for sale in the Smiling Hill Farm retail store, as well as restaurants and shops in Portland and Midcoast Maine.[91]

Silvery Moon Creamery is housed at Smiling Hill Farm, just seven miles west of downtown Portland, where the landscape quickly dissipates into scenic countryside. The three-hundred-year-old dairy farm sits on top of a hill, complete with a red dairy barn, a large pond filled with ducks and a field of cows. These cows produce the milk that is packaged in Smiling Hill's signature glass bottles reminiscent of a milkman's delivery.

The dairy plant and cheese room sit right next to the road on which cars speed out of Portland, but it's quiet inside the clean, white, sealed cheese room. Grimm and Renaud are concerned with introducing undesirable bacteria that could potentially ruin their products. They wear scrubs and hairnets and wash their hands and arms frequently, like doctors scrubbing into surgery.

When asked what's special about making cheese in Maine, Grimm points to the specific conditions of any cheesemaking operation: "The cheese we make here is unique because of what the cows eat here, the germs that they're exposed to and then the work that we put in. The bacteria we have growing in our aging cave is all very unique."[92]

Dorothee Grimm and Tyler Renaud have been at the helm of the creamery for the last two years. Previously, Grimm worked in microbiology in Montana, and Renaud cooked in several Portland restaurants. With Grimm's knowledge of harnessing the transformative power of bacteria and Renaud's long-standing connections with local purveyors, the two make Silvery Moon's traditional-style cheeses with a local twist.

An Alpine-style Tomme is washed with Portland's Rising Tide Brewing Company's Ishmael, an American copper ale, and aged for months. Casco Bay Dulse is a fresh feta-like cheese, pressed with a layer of local dried red seaweed flakes, imparting a hint of salt to the slightly sweet cheese. Slices from small rounds of Brie and Camembert tingle on your tongue with acidity and finish with a creamy, buttery texture. Squeaky cheddar cheese curds are sold to restaurants, where they're served melted over fries with gravy in poutine, a traditional French Canadian dish.[93]

One of seventy-three licensed cheesemakers in the state, Silvery Moon Creamery is a midsized operation based on production. The smallest cheesemaker may heat five gallons of milk at a time in her home kitchen, and the largest, four-thousand-acre Pineland Farms in New Gloucester, is capable of heating several thousand gallons of milk at a time.[94] While producing less cheese overall than other well-known cheesemaking states like Wisconsin and Vermont, Maine has the fastest-growing number of licensed cheesemakers in the country.[95]

Cheesemaker and president of the Maine Cheese Guild Eric Rector says the reason for the industry's growth and recognition is simple: "Maine produces some of the best milk in the world, in my opinion. In addition, dairy regulations in the state allow the retail sale of raw fluid milk of the highest quality, giving every Maine cheesemaker, especially those who don't milk their own herds, access to excellent examples of this crucial ingredient."[96]

Grimm says the resources of the Maine Cheese Guild contribute to the high concentration of cheesemakers in Maine. The guild provided her education in cheesemaking when she took two hands-on workshops from

Tomme cheese is aged at Silvery Moon Creamery in a climate-controlled cheese cave. Some wheels are washed with local beer to create a flavored rind. *Photo by Greta Rybus.*

well-established cheesemakers before starting at Silvery Moon Creamery.[97] In addition to classes, the guild promotes Maine cheese by coordinating public educational events like Open Creamery Day, where the public can tour participating creameries.

Once a year, the American Cheese Society (ACS) holds its annual conference and competition, and the Maine Cheese Guild helps cheesemakers attend by subsidizing conference fees and travel costs. The guild also pays for a large shipment of cheese to be sent to the competition so Maine cheesemakers can participate even if they aren't in attendance. In 2013, five Maine cheesemakers placed in the competition, and Silvery Moon Creamery's provolone won second place—the first ACS award for Grimm and Renaud.[98]

Above: Scenic Smiling Hill Farm on the western edge of Portland has been owned by the Knight family for more than three hundred years. *Photo by Greta Rybus.*

Left: Winter Hill Farm yogurt and local cheese for sale at Rosemont Market & Bakery. *Photo by Kate McCarty.*

Smiling Hill is one of a handful of dairy farms left in Cumberland County; fewer than three hundred dairy farms remain in the state.[99] Farms go out of business as older generations retire or because the business is no longer profitable. Maine's convoluted milk pricing system means that, at times, farmers are paid less than the cost of production for their milk. The State of Maine established the Maine Milk Pool, a subsidy fund, to help cover the cost of production when milk prices are low. Because Smiling Hill bottles its own milk, the farm avoids some of the obstacles other dairy farmers face when they sell milk to processors.[100]

While selling fluid milk may be a losing proposition, artisanal handmade cheese can fetch a much higher retail price. Dairy farmers frequently turn to cheesemaking as a way to add value to their product, as is the case at Winter Hill Farm in Freeport. The farm recently changed hands when the previous farmers retired, and the land was purchased by two families looking to preserve farmland in southern Maine. The landowners found a couple to manage the farm and worked with them to sell a conservation easement to the Freeport Conservation Trust.[101]

Farmers Steve Burger and Sarah Wiederkehr inherited a herd of twenty Randall cows, a rare breed historically used for milk and meat and as draft animals. Now in their third year of managing the farm, Wiederkehr and Burger raise pigs and produce raw milk, yogurt, cheese and vegetables. Like so many other local producers, Wiederkehr sees the demand for her product growing every year. "People are just mad for good-quality artisanal cheeses," she says. "Previously, local cheese options were pretty limited, and when you're making giant batches, it compromises a bit of the handmade quality that comes with batches of artisanal cheeses."[102]

As a new cheesemaker, Wiederkehr experiments with cheeses that she enjoys making while balancing customer demand with cheeses that produce well. She makes six or seven cheeses regularly, including Camembert, Cambozola (a blue cheese with a bloomy rind), feta and an ashed bloomy-rind cheese. Wiederkehr says, "The bloomy blue is a lot of effort, and it's a little bit finicky, but I love it. I've come to this realization that I really like making the bloomy-rind cheeses—I like to see things grow."[103]

On the day I visit, Wiederkehr is preparing the cheese room to produce a small batch of the Cambozola. She sprays out her stainless steel equipment with a hose while her employee bottles milk in an adjacent room. She uses whatever milk is left over after the milk orders are filled to make cheese. In winter, when the cows are grain-fed, there may be only fifteen to twenty gallons of milk left. In the spring and summer, when the cows are pastured, they can produce an extra fifty gallons a day to be used for cheesemaking.[104]

Winter Hill Farm's products are available at local farmers' markets and shops, including Rosemont Market. Last year, Wiederkehr and Burger embraced several opportunities for cheese tastings, pairings and on-the-farm dinners. Partnering with Rosemont Market, they offered a "Terroir of Dairy" dinner in August, featuring a milk tasting and a meal of veal and other farm-fresh products.[105]

Figuring that those who are attracted to small batches of beer would also be attracted to small batches of cheese, Winter Hill Farm's cheese was included in a pairing with Rising Tide Brewing Company's beer during Portland Beer Week in the fall. "I like the personal face-to-face time of events and at farmers' markets," says Wiederkehr. "I think if we had just put our cheeses in wholesale accounts, they wouldn't have sold as well. It's predominately people that have met us and know us that are buying our cheese."[106]

With a burgeoning farmers' market scene in southern Maine, support from the Maine Cheese Guild and plenty of interested customers, the Maine cheese industry stands to continue to grow. Larger creameries like Silvery Moon widely distribute their cheeses, while smaller operations like Winter Hill Farm rely on personal connections to flourish. Fortunately, the market for Maine-made cheese is far from saturated, as demand grows and cheesemakers explore the expansive world of cheese.

Chapter 8

FARMING THE SEA

Maine Shellfish

The opening of Eventide Oyster Co. in June 2012 marked the beginning of an oyster renaissance in Portland. Local oysters served on the half shell can be found at plenty of restaurants in town, but Eventide offers the most expansive selection with upward of twenty varieties available, half of them from Maine. In making so many oysters available, Eventide has helped to advance diners' appreciation of different oyster varieties. When tasting metallic Belons, the last wild oyster species in North America; small, sweet Beausoleils from New Brunswick, Canada; or briny Winter Points from Bath, the differences in oysters' tastes are apparent.

Oysters have always grown in Maine, with evidence of oyster fans among several communities of American Indians in the Midcoast area. Along the shores of the Damariscotta River, huge piles of oyster shells, or middens, are visible. Thousands of years ago, oysters grew naturally in Maine's estuaries, growing shells up to twenty inches long.[107] Wild oyster populations declined in the late 1800s due to changes in water temperature.[108] Now, the Eastern oyster is cultivated in bags that float just under the surface of the water from Mount Desert Island's Penobscot Bay to Portland's Casco Bay.

Most every oyster grown on the East Coast is the same species, with the differences in taste resulting from their habitat. Oysters grown in Maine tend to thrive in cold, deep waters that don't freeze in the wintertime. As a result, Maine Eastern oysters are small, with deeply cupped shells, and are typically brinier than those grown in other regions.

Another species of oysters is found in sporadic pockets off the Maine coast. In the late 1950s, scientists tried to replenish oyster populations with a hardy species from Europe. The European Flat oyster thrives in the rivers of Brittany, France, in a similar climate to that of Maine. Called "Belons" when originating in France, these oysters are large, with shallow shells and a distinctly metallic taste.

Abigail Carroll of Nonesuch Oysters first tasted true Belons while living in Paris, France, five years ago. Originally from Maine, Carroll moved to Paris and was working as a stock trader. But when a nagging feeling that something was missing got the better of her, she moved back to Maine and pondered her next move. Here she met a new friend who was interested in starting an aquaculture business.

Having no interest in the dirty work of oyster farming, Carroll lent her financial skills to help write a business plan and invested startup funds. But the would-be farmer turned out not to be as invested as Carroll, and she quickly found that rather than act as a silent partner, she was now the sole proprietor of an oyster farm. Deciding to make the best of it, Carroll now spends her time harvesting oysters, cleaning equipment and tending to spat, or baby oysters, in their "nursery."

On a bright day in late July, Carroll showed me around her oyster farm or aquaculture lease site. She leases two sites from the State of Maine in the Scarborough River, where the fresh river water flows to the Atlantic Ocean, forming the Saco Bay. This quick-moving estuary provides the perfect habitat for growing a unique oyster, one that is defined by its *meroir*—or *terroir* of the sea. Just as the characteristics of soil impart a sense of place to wine grapes, the environments in which the same species of oyster is raised impart wholly different flavors to each individual oyster.[109]

"You can't [just] talk about a Nonesuch oyster," Carroll says as we overlook her site composed of black mesh bags filled with oysters, held afloat by black foam blocks. "We've got the ground seed and the stuff growing in bags, and all of these oysters are very different."[110] After Carroll expertly shucks a Nonesuch oyster that grew in a bag floating just under the surface of the water for me to try, it tastes distinctly different than the "free range" oyster in the algae-covered shell that she plucked from the bottom of the river.

While eighty shellfish aquaculture lease sites totaling close to 650 acres produce millions of oysters per year in Maine, *meroir* is expressed differently in oysters grown even only a few feet apart.[111] This expression of place through flavor gave Carroll the idea to create the Maine Oyster Tasting Trail, and

Abigail Carroll of Nonesuch Oysters checks the bags containing her oysters growing in the Scarborough River. *Photo by Kate McCarty.*

through this she hopes to "inspire people to go up and down the Maine coast [tasting oysters] like you might go to Napa Valley and taste wines."[112]

Carroll envisions oyster lovers traveling from the Scarborough River in southern Maine north to the Damariscotta River, where two-thousand-year-old oyster middens line the riverbanks. Here, you can taste briny oysters with a clean finish imparted by the cold, deep waters in which the oysters thrive. You could spend a fair amount of time in Damariscotta sampling oysters from the twenty-one producers in the area, each expressing its own *meroir*.

Currently, however, Maine oyster farmers are not legally permitted to sell their products directly at their lease sites. Instead, farmers sell to wholesalers, who sell to retailers, where customers can then purchase their local oysters. For those customers wishing to come to the waterfront, see the oyster farm and learn from the farmer—for a Maine Oyster Tasting Trail to really take shape—legislation needs to be changed to allow for the sale of shellfish at aquaculture lease sites.

"The equivalent situation would be you show up at Napa Valley, you taste some incredible red wine that you just think is delicious and then they tell you to go to the supermarket and buy a bottle," laments Carroll.[113] She's

Maine boasts a variety of oysters, seen here for sale at Harbor Fish Market. *Photo by Kate McCarty.*

Bangs Island Mussels are sold at Harbor Fish Market, a few wharves away from its waterfront operation. *Photo by Kate McCarty.*

working with her local state representative to modify these laws in order to take advantage of the ever-growing food tourism market.

While fishermen have long since worked with local governments to lobby for legislation that benefits their livelihood, Carroll represents a different type of sea farmer—one that doesn't necessarily come from a long generational line of fishermen. Carroll had no experience growing oysters when she started her business, so she's been working closely with scientists at the University of New England (UNE) in Biddeford to learn the industry.[114]

Carroll and the UNE aquaculture department are specifically working on breeding oysters in captivity. Most oyster farmers purchase baby oysters that are sterile, so the oysters don't ever waste energy on reproduction. When oysters reproduce, the taste and texture change in an undesirable way. This gives rise to the maxim "only eat oysters in months that have an *r*." But purchasing oysters is a considerable expense for an oyster farmer, so Carroll is hoping to successfully breed oysters in captivity.

While Carroll uses the university's lab equipment and faculty knowledge and employs student interns, the students gain practical experience out on her farm. "These [students] at UNE don't necessarily have a shed full of tools and some of these other hands-on skills that maybe the lobstermen converting to oysters would have," Carroll explains. "I think it's been helpful to a lot of kids to come out here and see what we do." More than forty marine science students graduate from UNE every year, and many will find a living working at one of the rising number of aquaculture farms in southern Maine, in particular at Nonesuch Oysters.[115]

With the increasing popularity of local foods like oysters, Carroll's business is sure to grow. To meet the demand, she is looking to expand her facilities, improve harvesting equipment and create new marketing opportunities. Although she calls herself an "accidental oyster farmer," Carroll has embraced this happy accident, to the benefit of all oyster lovers.

The cool waters of Casco Bay also provide the perfect habitat for mussels. Mussels grow wild in shallow water near the rocky shoreline and are frequently exposed at low tide. These wild mussels are harvested by hand or by dredge, but they take longer to grow and are not always of the highest quality. Rope-cultured mussels, on the other hand, grow quickly and produce large, plump, sweet mussels. By suspending mussels in the water column, the rope culture system helps avoid the pitfalls of wild mussels: being buried by sediment and being eaten by any number of predators. As a result, the happy, protected mussels grow much faster and are ready for market in eighteen months instead of several years.[116]

Just off the rocky islands of Portland's Casco Bay, Bangs Island Mussels grows rope-cultured mussels that have become beloved by chefs for their plump, sweet meat. Behind Bangs Island and Clapboard Island, three forty-by forty-foot rafts made of plastic floats and wooden decking quietly sway in the ocean current. Suspended from the rafts is a series of thirty-five-foot ropes that total one mile in length. On these ropes grow tens of thousands of pounds of two-inch-long blue-black mussels.[117]

Rope-culturing mussels has its own set of hurdles, including predators and weather conditions that can break rafts or disrupt harvesting. Seeding, cleaning, maintaining the rafts and harvesting the mussels is labor-intensive work. But the simplicity of their operation surprises even company owner Matt Moretti. "We're just helping nature do the best job it can," he says one afternoon as we overlook the Portland Harbor from the dock outside his mussel processing plant on the wharf.[118]

Moretti and his father, Gary, purchased Bangs Island Mussels from Tollef Olson and Paul Dobbins, who had been running the business for ten years. Olson and Dobbins went on to found Ocean Approved, selling kelp products like pickles and noodles.[119] The Morettis expanded the business by adding more rafts, ropes and harvesting equipment to increase production. Moretti and his father were attracted to the sustainability of mussel farming, seeing themselves more as "facilitators" than farmers. But like all aquaculture operations, the work is physical and repetitive.

Working year round, Bangs Island Mussels employees strip mussels from the ropes using equipment mounted onboard their harvesting barge. The mussels are then brought to the processing plant, where they are cleaned, sorted, bagged and sold to their wholesaler. Bangs Island Mussels are shipped to chefs all over the country and are served in Portland at Fore Street, Hugo's, Eventide Oyster Co. and Five Fifty-Five and are available fresh at Harbor Fish Market and Browne Trading Company.[120]

Whether they're steamed with wine and chive butter, wood-roasted with vermouth and almond butter or poached in an *escabeche* and served with grilled bread and chorizo, Portland chefs prepare these fresh mussels simply, to let the sweet, rich flavor of the meat shine through.

In a world of dire seafood stories, aquaculture projects Bangs Island Mussels and Nonesuch Oysters are refreshing tales of ingenuity and sustainability. Aquaculturists like Moretti and Carroll are working hard to grow shellfish that express a true sense of place. In the hands of talented chefs and shuckers, these jewels of the sea offer a true taste of Maine waters.

Chapter 9
LOBSTER

A Coastal Delicacy

O f course, the first food people think of when they think of Maine is lobster. And for good reason—in 2013, Maine lobstermen harvested 125.9 million pounds of lobster, worth $364.5 million and representing 90 percent of the world's supply.[121] On Portland's waterfront Commercial Street, nearly every restaurant serves lobster. Your options for lobster in Portland are comprehensive: steamed lobster, baked lobster, lobster chowder, lobster rolls, lobster salad, lobster linguini…the Holy Donut even offered a lobster donut for a while.

DiMillo's floating restaurant (housed in a renovated car ferry) serves classic steamed lobster dinners and offers a special twin lobster dinner for twenty-six dollars. On the other end of Commercial Street, Boone's Fish House & Oyster Room, the newest restaurant from Chef Harding Lee Smith, serves baked stuffed lobster and a tableside lobster bake, complete with hard-boiled eggs and kielbasa. Lobster is featured in no fewer than eight menu items at the iconic raw bar J's Oyster. Ten of the twelve restaurants on Commercial Street serve lobster rolls.

But if you ask a local where to order the best lobster dinner in Portland, you'll frequently hear that they don't know. Most locals buy their lobsters live and then steam them at home. Some will even scoff that lobsters should only be eaten in the privacy of your home, where you can get covered in butter and lobster juices without an audience.

One of the most unique ways to get a lobster dinner in Portland is to go out on the boat that catches it first. At Lucky Catch Lobster Tours, you can take a ninety-minute boat ride, help stuff smelly herring into bait bags, hold live lobsters and learn about Portland Harbor and its lobster fishing industry. Commercial fisherman Tom Martin started the business in 1996 when the state began to decrease the number of traps allowed per lobstering license. Anticipating the loss of his business's financial viability, Martin decided to diversify by taking tourists out on lobster cruises. Now Lucky Catch has two boats in Portland Harbor, both of which offer tours in the summer and fish for lobster in the winter.[122]

On a warm day in early October, Lucky Catch captain Dave Lalibertie and sternman Brian Rapp lead a tour of fifteen passengers. After welcoming us aboard their

Bite Into Maine's picnic-style lobster roll is a pound of tail and claw meat, tossed with melted butter and served in a toasted split-top bun. *Photo by Kate McCarty.*

sparkling-clean, open-deck lobster boat, Lalibertie slowly drives us out of the wharf past DiMillo's restaurant, a lazy harbor seal and marinas full of sailboats and lobster boats.

Across the harbor, the sun highlights the slowly changing fall leaves of Peaks Island, and in the distance, the Portland Head Light flashes steadily, marking the end of Casco Bay and the beginning of the Atlantic Ocean. We turn away from the ocean, driving farther into the bay, where brightly colored lobster buoys mark a line of lobster traps under water between the rocky islands.

While Rapp narrates the life of a lobster in Casco Bay, Lalibertie pulls the thirty-seven-foot boat alongside a colorful buoy, scoops it up and wraps it around a hydraulic winch. Putting the engine into neutral, he winds the winch until the muddy lobster trap comes to the surface of the water. After hauling the trap aboard and balancing it on the gunnel, he invites us to see what he's caught.

Several small lobsters wave their antennae at us from inside the green metal trap. Lalibertie opens a small door in the side of the trap, deftly grabs a lobster by its shell and holds it up for us all to admire. Live lobsters' shells are a beautiful mottled combination of brown, green, orange and red, highlighted to blend in with the rocks and sea grass at the bottom of the ocean.

Demonstrating the legal size required to keep a lobster, Lalibertie uses a small metal tool called a culling iron to measure the lobster's carapace. In order to be a legal catch, a lobster must be larger than three and a half inches from its eye socket to the end of its shell. This minimum size requirement is to protect the next generation of breeding lobsters. Lobsters larger than five inches are considered "breeders" and are thrown back as well. Due to regulations like these, the Maine lobster industry is a sustainable, well-managed one. Every year, lobstermen see an increase in lobster stocks.[123]

After determining that none of the lobsters in the trap are keepers, Lalibertie frees our catch and restocks the bait bag before pushing the trap off the boat. We repeat the process several times, making a big loop around some of the scenic attractions of Casco Bay, including Fort Gorges, a Civil War–era fort.

Once we are tied up securely at the dock, one couple on the tour decides to purchase live lobsters for dinner. Rapp selects two from the tank of keepers onboard and hands dinner over to the couple, who gingerly accept the crustaceans. The couple, holding the lobsters at arm's length, heads up the ramp to Portland Lobster Company. The pier-side restaurant will steam and serve the lobsters with drawn butter and sides for ten dollars.

Portland's lobster industry is inevitably entwined with tourism, as 4 million people visit Portland each year, many of them looking to eat lobster. Rapp and Lalibertie see their summertime work as helping to promote the lobster industry. "Whether we are doing tours or commercial fishing, it is a rough way to make a living," says Lalibertie. "I think most people have an appreciation for these tours because we are educating people about the lobster industry."[124]

Lobsters haven't always been considered the delicacy they are today. In fact, they used to be so plentiful in Maine waters that American Indians and colonists were able to catch them by hand in the shallows. The crustaceans were so abundant that they were used as bait and fertilizer and fed to prisoners and indentured servants.[125]

By the time Maine seceded from Massachusetts in 1820, the population of European settlers was well established, and innovations in lobstering advanced quickly. Driven by increasing demand in Boston and New York,

Live lobsters' coloring helps them blend into the ocean floor; their shell's red color emerges after steaming. *Photo by Greta Rybus.*

Maine lobsters are caught in traps specifically designed to allow lobsters to escape should the traps be lost. *Photo by Greta Rybus.*

lobstermen began to use wooden traps to catch lobsters. The use of sailing smacks helped to transport the perishable catch to shore more efficiently. Smack boats are small sailboats with a cargo hold full of circulating sea water. Lobstermen sold their catch to smackmen who would, in turn, transport it to shore, allowing the lobstermen to continue to fish.[126]

In the mid-1800s, canning became a popular way to increase consumers' access to Maine lobster. Burnham & Morrill Company opened its first packing plant on Franklin Street in Portland, canning lobster, corn and eventually baked beans. By 1880, canned lobster had become so popular that production and sales of canned lobster surpassed those of live lobster.[127] Around the turn of the century, lobster populations began to decrease as the number of lobstermen exploded, driven by the profitable canning business. Fearing a loss of industry, the state passed the first conservation laws, including a size minimum and a ban on keeping egg-bearing females in 1872 and 1874, respectively.[128]

As soon as the canning industry became widespread, the railroad system expanded into Maine. The arrival of the Grand Trunk Railroad in Portland made the shipping of live lobster packed in ice possible. Restrictions imposed on the canning and fishing industries by the government in World War I further contributed to the decline of canned lobster.[129] In the 1940s, Burnham & Morrill Company discontinued canning lobster and focused on frozen foods and its brick-oven baked beans.[130]

While lobster was previously widely available across the country, it took government rationing during World War II to create an appreciation within middle-class households. With incomes bolstered by the wartime economy and a shortage of other proteins, lobster became a popular mealtime choice. In the latter half of the twentieth century, Maine's burgeoning tourist economy further promoted lobster to a status symbol dish rather than a poor man's food.[131]

Today, the demand for Maine lobster is greater than ever, with increasingly advanced technology making the shipping of live lobsters possible worldwide.[132] Thanks to Maine's strict conservation policies, the supply of lobster is also higher than ever.[133] But paradoxically, lobstermen have recently been struggling to make a living catching lobster.

Lobster is one of the few foods for which the price is determined by supply and demand, and a recent glut of lobsters caused low wholesale prices for Maine lobstermen. Lobsterman Alex Curtis fishes in Penobscot Bay from North Haven, and he remembers a wholesale price or "boat price" of less than two dollars per pound last year. When Curtis began fishing, in the late '90s, the boat price was near seven dollars per pound.[134]

The B&M cannery on Portland's Casco Bay now makes baked beans but used to can lobster during the late 1800s. *Photo by Corey Templeton.*

Climate change, in particular warming water, is thought to have caused the recent glut in lobster landings. More lobsters are moving farther north and are thought to be facing less predation by other species as Maine's waters warm.[135] In 2013, a low boat price coupled with historic numbers of lobster landings meant that lobster boat captains were struggling to make a profit from their daily operations.

The Maine Lobster Collaborative, a marketing initiative, was established that same year to counteract the glut in the market.[136] Locals were encouraged to buy more lobster as a sort of patriotic duty. With a whole live lobster costing about four dollars, it was easy to comply. Lobster landings and prices have stabilized recently, with wholesalers paying lobstermen over three dollars per pound.

Lobstering is an extremely lucrative occupation in Maine; some captains earn up to $1,000 per day in the height of the season. But before you decide to quit your day job and take up a life at sea, know that lobstering licenses are extremely hard to come by. A set number of licenses is issued, and one must complete a two-year apprenticeship with a licensed captain before becoming eligible for a license.[137]

Like many things, lobstering in southern Maine is very different than it is farther up the coast. Rapp and Lalibertie of Lucky Catch have to fish farther offshore than North Haven lobstermen like Curtis. From Portland, lobstermen

Lobster prices change frequently, depending on the season. Wintertime prices at Harbor Fish Market in Portland are relatively high. *Photo by Kate McCarty.*

may have to steam hours out into the ocean to set their traps. Starting fifteen miles from the mainland on an island like North Haven in Penobscot Bay, you're already well into the state's most productive lobstering grounds.

Unlike some of the other species of local seafood, Maine lobster is a well-managed industry, supporting many families in coastal communities from Kittery to Lubec. As climate change, Maine's aging population and licensing management issues shape the industry, its practices will change. But lobstering is an important cultural and economic force in Maine and is prioritized as such by the state's leaders.

The experience of eating a Maine lobster can be as varied as seeing the process from trap-to-table with Lucky Catch Lobster Tours, simply ordering a lobster roll in a Portland restaurant or enjoying a traditional lobster bake from an oceanfront fire pit. The city's talented chefs churn out as many lobster creations as they can dream up, pairing the sweet, delicate meat with light, summery flavors or folding it into rich, comforting dishes. Gone are the days when lobstermen's children would trade their lobster roll lunches for peanut butter and jelly sandwiches. The once humble lobster has become a tourist attraction in its own right, and there's plenty to be had in our city by the sea.

Chapter 10

A FISH STORY

Sustainability and Gulf of Maine Seafood

Fishermen have long since made a living in Maine pulling haddock, cod, flounder and swordfish from surrounding waters. The Gulf of Maine, a large bay encompassing all of Maine's shoreline and stretching from Cape Cod to Nova Scotia, is home to more than two thousand species and is considered one of the world's richest marine resources. Due to the area's unique geography, ocean currents and water depth, the Gulf of Maine is a feeding ground for many marine animals. These specific conditions attract species from bottom-dwelling lobsters to migrating humpback whales.[138]

Fishing has played a vital part in the development and economy of the state for thousands of years. The Wabanaki Indians and the first English settlers fished with hand lines from canoes and schooners in the late 1600s. The Gulf of Maine's bountiful seafood populations enabled English settlers to survive the harsh winters of a developing colony with limited resources.

The available fishing technologies of the eighteenth and nineteenth centuries dictated a sustainable rate of harvesting.[139] Changes in fishing technology, like diesel-powered engines and more efficient trawl nets, allowed fishermen to increase their harvests and their profits. The North Atlantic cod population crashed notably in the 1990s, and strict management and conservation policies were enacted to protect the species. National management of fishing industries didn't occur until the 1980s.[140]

But overfishing alone does not account for the decline in groundfish populations. The world's oceans are changing—warming and acidifying—with unforeseen consequences on regional species. Maine fishermen no

Smelt is yet another popular fish species whose populations are declining. The small fish are caught in the wintertime and are usually breaded and pan-fried. *Photo by Kate McCarty.*

longer have the luxury of high quotas and abundant populations of many species of groundfish.

With local fish populations in various states of decline and recovery, government and nonprofit research organizations are working together to achieve sustainability for the Gulf of Maine's fisheries. Researchers study the effects of conservation measures on seafood populations while promoting other species that now call the Gulf of Maine home. Fishermen are diversifying their operations by changing their gear to catch new species. Changing demand for specific seafood species takes time, but many programs and initiatives in Portland are dedicated to preserving our marine resources.

The sustainable seafood programs of Portland's Gulf of Maine Research Institute (GMRI) aim to lessen the economic blow of fisheries management by promoting local seafood species with healthy populations. Sustainable Seafood Programs manager Jen Levin works with restaurants and retailers to certify and brand Gulf of Maine Responsibly Harvested Seafood. This seal assures consumers that a particular product has healthy populations, is caught using environmentally sensitive practices and supports shoreside processing and distribution infrastructure.[141]

Seafood caught in the Gulf of Maine is frequently shipped overseas for processing before being shipped back for sale in the United States. Sustainable seafood must not only be from healthy populations but also support the communities in the Gulf of Maine's watershed. GMRI's branding program assures customers that their seafood supports many facets of their community's economy. Gulf of Maine Responsibly Harvested products are sold in local grocery stores Hannaford and Shaw's and by waterfront seafood processors Cozy Harbor, Bristol Seafood and North Atlantic Seafood.

In addition, GMRI partnered with Delhaize America, Hannaford supermarket's parent company, in 2009 to ensure that all its stores' seafood met standards for sustainability. The company's policy requires traceability and only buys from suppliers that meet third-party standards (like GMRI's) for responsibly harvesting and farming methods.[142] By 2012, all of the company's 1,700 stores in New England were in compliance with this seafood policy.[143]

After helping establish sustainable seafood in all Delhaize America stores, Levin turned to her attention to growing GMRI's Culinary Partners program. The program educates participating restaurants' staff about local sustainably harvested seafood. Levin sees this work as necessary to establish a strong market for Gulf of Maine seafood and to support the people depending on the industry. She explains how GMRI's programs "look at both the ecologic sustainability and the economic sustainability to make sure that there are market forces in place that enable the fishing community, and the processing and distribution communities, to thrive."[144] Levin sees consumer awareness of local and sustainably harvested seafood as a precursor for lasting change.

Serving Sustainably

With such a thriving restaurant scene, Portland chefs and restaurateurs stand well positioned to influence diners' tastes. In becoming a GMRI Culinary Partner, a restaurant agrees to always have Gulf of Maine seafood on its menu, be it lobster, mussels, cod or scallops. GMRI trains restaurant staff about local seafood and provides educational materials, while the restaurants pledge to improve their businesses' environmental sustainability. Currently, five restaurants participate in the program, and Levin hopes to have forty enrolled by the end of the year.[145]

For the past three years, GMRI organized Out of the Blue, a program funded by a NOAA Fisheries grant to promote underutilized species from the Gulf of Maine. These species were identified by factors like low boat price, overseas value, well-established management practices and abundant populations. Out of the Blue promoted five species: dogfish, redfish, mackerel, whiting and pollock. GMRI hosted regular meetings with fishermen, chefs and other food service providers, like Bowdoin College, to discuss issues surrounding the use of these underutilized species.[146]

Restaurants and other food service providers that participated in the promotion showcased the featured fish on their menus for ten consecutive days once a month. The Salt Exchange served redfish with gnocchi, locally foraged ramps, wild mushrooms and fresh parsley. Hot Suppa put its Cajun spin on smoked Atlantic mackerel, serving it for breakfast in hash topped with fried eggs. Five Fifty-Five showcased dogfish poached in olive oil, tomatoes and fresh herbs.

The Salt Exchange owner Charlie Bryon was a member of the program's steering committee and participated in the program for the three years it ran. He felt that the promotion was a rare opportunity that benefited his customers, the fishing community, the environment and his business simultaneously. Bryon explains that restaurants are always looking to use underappreciated cuts of meat or fish. If the product isn't popular with chefs, it will be inexpensive, resulting in higher profit margins for the restaurant.

Bryon points to hanger steak, once considered a subpar cut but now a favorite with home cooks and in Portland restaurants like Fore Street and the Grill Room. "I hate to be that transparent, but that's what restaurants do," Bryon says. "Things become popular in the food industry because they're showcased by restaurants." By showcasing unpopular but abundant local fish, Bryon hopes to play a part in increasing the demand for these species.[147]

The Out of the Blue program received a lot of media attention and exposed diners to fish they might not have tried otherwise. But during the program's execution, GMRI's Levin witnessed the hurdles that face changing consumer demand. She describes a "vicious cycle" between fishermen and chefs that keeps underutilized species out of restaurants: "Fishermen don't handle [these fish] well because the price is so low, but the high-end markets don't want it because it isn't handled well."[148]

Fishermen and chefs rarely communicate with one another about available fish and desired products. Rather, a seafood distributor like

Wild and farm-raised fresh fish for sale at Harbor Fish Market. *Photo by Kate McCarty.*

Harbor Fish Market acts as the go-between. The seafood markets purchase whole fish from fishermen, break them down and sell the filets to restaurants. Chefs typically ask their seafood purveyors what's available, while fishermen catch and sell the markets fish that's profitable and in demand. As a result, only a relative few species of local fish are sold in markets and served at restaurants.[149]

According to Levin, this cycle occurs because of a lack of communication. She says, "The middle guys will say, even if a fisherman brought in a hundred pounds of mackerel, 'I'm not going to buy it because no one is asking for it.' Restaurants ask the dealers what's available, and it's not available because no one is asking for it." Part of GMRI's work is encouraging communication between the suppliers and the restaurant industry.[150]

Chef Damian Sansonetti of Piccolo witnessed the issue firsthand when trying to source mackerel for his restaurant. "I'd been begging my seafood purveyor for mackerel, but the problem is you're in a fishing town and a lot of mackerel goes for bait," he said. He finally acquired a small portion. "They were like three little fish, so we cut them up and made a nice little crudo. It was so clean, so pristine," he said. He served the mackerel at his restaurant's Sunday Supper with lemon zest, lemon, toasted pine nuts and slices of fresh Calabrian chiles.[151]

At his restaurants, Chef Masa Miyake recently shifted the focus of the menus from traditional Japanese products to more local seafood. His business partner, Will Garfield, explains how they're "slowly moving away from some of the Japanese imports as far as specialty fish."[152] Instead, he's finding local substitutes to serve in his three Portland restaurants. Garfield adds, "We can get monkfish liver in Maine, so why not focus on that instead of bringing in Spanish mackerel? The Northern New England whelk, which is a bycatch from lobsters, looks like an oversized periwinkle."[153]

Garfield credits the great relationships he has with local purveyors for helping him to acquire these local products. ISF Trading harvests local sea urchin and typically ships its product to Japan. But Garfield is able to purchase fresh, unpasteurized urchin directly from the seafood processor. With the new seafood sources, he hopes to provide a distinct sense of place for the customer. "We try to create unique atmospheres in all of our restaurants, but the focus has got to be the food and always will remain that way."[154]

A Fresh Take on Local Fish

When Justine Simon and her husband, Marty Odlin, moved to Portland so Odlin could join his family's fishing business, Simon surely predicted that she'd be eating a lot of local fish. But what she didn't foresee is that the abundance of fresh fish in her life would lead to her own business that also supports the fishing industry.

After tasting the fresh fish that Odlin's work yielded, Simon had a revelation. "I just noticed a really big difference between the kind of fish I was eating with his family and what was available to me in the stores," Simon says. She saw an opportunity to diversify her family's income while connecting local food lovers directly with the local fishermen. She decided to put her past experience working in food systems to work in the Portland area. As a result, Salt + Sea Community Supported Fishery (CSF) now delivers fresh seafood and shellfish shares to one hundred customers.[155]

The "community supported" model is a popular way for people in Portland to eat local food and support area farmers. Typically, CSA customers buy shares in early spring that are then delivered throughout a specified season. Farmers use the upfront capital to plant, upgrade and repair before the cash-generating crops come in, while the customer is guaranteed a varied supply of fresh, local food.

Portlanders have more than 150 options for farm shares during the growing season, with several winter options too. Applying the CSA model to seafood, Simon offers two-month shares of in-season fresh fish and shellfish.[156]

Simon buys whole fish direct from fishermen and stores the fish in a brined ice solution. Salt + Sea employees then cut the fish into filets for shares on the day of their delivery. Storing the whole fish in a solution of ice and salt water gives the fish cutters flexibility to purchase fish all week long and still cut it fresh the day it's delivered to their customers. "Cutting day of delivery is really unheard of in the industry. It's such a perishable product. It's just a really important principle to us," Simon says.[157]

Simon cites the statistic that 90 percent of fish consumed in the United States is imported. "Even in a place like Portland, where the fishery has historically been such a huge part of the economy," she says, "you go into the store and it's a lot of imported fish—a lot of imported haddock, even though haddock is really abundant right now." Even if it's caught nearby, fish is frequently frozen at sea and shipped to China for cutting. Then, Simon says, "There's a lot of soaking in chemicals to keep the texture and consistency okay because you're freezing and thawing it."[158] For someone looking to eat local or to take advantage of the plentiful seafood in the Gulf of Maine, this process isn't appealing for many reasons.

While Portland offers many options for buying fresh, locally caught fish, few offer the unexpected variety of a CSF. Just like having to learn how to prepare and serve unfamiliar vegetables that come in your CSA share, Salt + Sea CSF customers may find themselves receiving less popular species of seafood like skate wing and whiting. Simon shares preparation tips and recipes in a daily newsletter and lets customers opt out of the species that are a more "acquired taste."[159]

Simon recalls the mixed reaction to one lesser-known species in particular:

> In New York, whiting is considered a real delicacy. But the whiting was our most divisive fish to date—I was getting e-mails from people saying they hated it, they never wanted to get it again. Most people just didn't want to deal with the whole fish. I e-mailed out to everyone reassuring them that we wouldn't offer it again, sorry that wasn't a hit, and I got like twenty e-mails back saying, "We loved it! We want it again!"[160]

Simon enjoys sharing the appeal of lesser-known species with her customers. She's working on developing a map of the Gulf of Maine to educate her customers on where the fish in their share is caught every day.[161]

In addition to the daily newsletter citing the fish's origin, Simon partnered with Wayside Food Programs operations manager Don Morrison to offer cooking classes, recently teaching participants how to prepare bacon-wrapped monkfish. She also donates shares that aren't picked up by her customers to the food rescue organization, where the filets can be frozen or turned into fish cakes to be served at one of their community meals.[162]

Many people like Simon are working hard to achieve sustainability within our local fisheries. Chefs, fishermen and organizations like GMRI strive to preserve our marine resources for the benefit of their own livelihoods and our community. While their work is not without significant hurdles, the benefits are apparent. Consumers are becoming more aware of the importance of supporting our local seafood industries. As this demand for sustainable food sources builds, perhaps even an underappreciated species like the once-maligned redfish will become the "hanger steak" of the seafood world.

Chapter 11

FISHMONGERS AND LOBSTER POUNDS

With so many seafood options in Portland, it might be easy to take such availability for granted. With so much of it available all over the country, regardless of proximity to the ocean, one could forget that the shipping of fresh fish is a relatively recent phenomenon. For those of us living in coastal Maine, where the sight, smell and sounds of the ocean are an ever-present part of one's day, it's even easier to consider fresh seafood as a given.

Two seafood markets on Portland's Commercial Street share few similarities past the selection of local seafood and their waterfront locations. One may be preferred over the other by some as an everyday market, and the other may seem more appropriate for a special occasion. At each market, you'll find cases of fresh seafood, displayed gently on crushed ice. Behind the scenes, two vastly different operations are taking place. Ultimately, both markets are dedicated to selling the highest-quality seafood they can find.

Browne Trading Company sits at the Western End of Commercial Street, the bright-blue exterior of its retail shop distracting the eye from the large brick building that houses its wholesale business. In fact, many locals don't know much more than the retail side of Browne Trading Company. The bright shop is full of local and gourmet products with just a few cases full of fresh fish and shellfish. Half of the shop's space is dedicated to a large selection of some of the finest wines available in the state.

Aside from the wine, none of the retail selections of smoked seafood, caviar and fresh fish displayed at Browne Trading Company are expansive.

The availability only hints at the huge quantities of seafood passing through the warehouse behind the retail store. When I ask store manager Chris Miller what kind of oysters are available that day, he lists the three types in the display case (two from Maine, one from Washington) but adds that there's more than five thousand oysters in the back, representing fifteen different varieties.[163]

The warehouse space behind the retail shop is a series of workspaces, all dedicated to different steps in the processing, packing and shipping of fresh seafood. Late on a Thursday afternoon, the intake and cutting rooms are empty of both people and fish. "This is a good sign," says Marketing Director Nick Branchina as we walk through an empty cooler. "That means we sold it all."[164] Thursdays are the busiest day in Browne Trading Company's warehouse as they receive shipments of fresh seafood from all over the world, purchase local seafood at the Portland Fish Exchange and fill and ship orders for the finest seafood restaurants in the country.

The next room is where all the action is taking place. Several men in aprons and knee-high boots are standing behind metal prep tables preparing seafood orders. Plastic pint containers of hand-harvested Maine diver scallops are labeled with order information, including the name of the diver. Filets of Australian tai snapper are packed into white wax-coated cardboard boxes filled with chipped ice. A man gently places live sea urchins into a box lined with foam to protect their delicate spikes during shipping. Completed orders labeled with abbreviations of high-end seafood restaurants in New York sit stacked on a pallet, waiting to be loaded onto a truck.

The quality of the seafood sold by Browne Trading Company is an obvious point of pride for the store's staff. Every step in their handling of the seafood is dedicated to selecting, adding or preserving quality. The company's founder, Rod Browne Mitchell, peruses the local catch at the fish auction every day, selecting only the highest-quality offerings. Skilled butchers break down these whole fish, producing pristine cuts. To ensure that quality isn't lost during transport, Mitchell developed the industry standard for shipping fresh fish.[165]

In fact, much of Mitchell's work in the last thirty years has shaped the way we think about seafood in our country. Mitchell got his start in Camden, Maine, with a serendipitous meeting of Chef Jean-Louis Palladin. Palladin befriended Mitchell in his wine and cheese shop, convincing him to source local seafood comparable to that of Palladin's native France. Mitchell used his local knowledge and connections to produce diver scallops, peekytoe crab and sea urchins. Chef Palladin introduced these products to the

Seafood orders for New York restaurants waiting to be shipped at Browne Trading Company. *Photo by Kate McCarty.*

wider world on his menu at the Watergate Hotel. Mitchell soon became the seafood purveyor to Palladin's friends Wolfgang Puck, Emeril Lagasse, Daniel Boulud and Eric Ripert.[166]

Mitchell moved his operation to the Portland waterfront in 1991, allowing him to participate in the daily fish auction. He also expanded his caviar selection and started buying farm-raised product from sustainable sources. Four years later, Mitchell added an in-house smoking operation. Smokehouses are common in the Midcoast Maine area, where many small coastal towns sit at the junction of a river and the ocean. Mitchell learned traditional cold-smoking methods in Camden and began producing beautiful smoked salmon using Daniel Boulud's recipe.[167]

What distinguishes Browne Trading Company is that you can purchase the same quality of fish in the retail shop that is also being served at Le Bernardin in New York. All of its seafood is of the same quality, regardless of the client. Chef Rob Evans says that he found Browne Trading

Atlantic salmon at Browne Trading Company is cured with salt, sugar and scotch whiskey before it's cold-smoked. *Photo by Kate McCarty.*

Company to be "a beacon of light" when he first moved to Portland in 2000. "They didn't even sell locally, didn't have locals buying their fish," he remembers.[168]

It may be true that locals don't see Browne Trading Company as the everyday seafood market in Portland. In a city with so many retail markets and restaurants providing great local seafood, such quality and abundance are taken for granted. It's the relative scarcity of quality seafood that makes Browne Trading Company's customers in New York and the South appreciate Maine products. But Mainers in the know seek out Rod Mitchell's products, whether it's a cut of local fish for dinner or a tin of caviar and fine wine for a special occasion.

To find the other popular Portland seafood market, walk east on Commercial Street from Browne Trading Company and take a right onto Custom House Wharf. The wharf is one of many that make up the city's working waterfront. At their Commercial Street ends, Portland's wharves house businesses that cater to tourists: restaurants, clothing boutiques and ice cream shops. But toward the water, their occupants quickly change into marine-related businesses: seafood processing plants, boatyards and the ferry terminal. This mixed-use zoning is mandated by a city ordinance that gives precedent to marine-related businesses on the waterfront.[169]

Many of Portland's wharves will give you the feeling that you're somewhere you're not supposed to be, in the presence of pickup trucks, boat jacks and forklifts. But Custom House Wharf, also home to the Porthole restaurant, a local favorite, feels more welcoming than others. And that's largely thanks to the presence of Harbor Fish Market. The market is easy to spot, with its signature red storefront, photographed and painted so often that the owners had the image trademarked.[170] The undulating roofline hints at the lifetime of the pier-side building, which has been a fish market since the 1800s.[171]

Inside, the market bustles with activity. Shoppers are picking out fish filets for the evening's dinner—local cod and haddock or imported Faroe Island salmon—and others are bagging up live Damariscotta River oysters or Bangs Island Mussels. All of the action is accompanied by the gurgling sounds of sea water as it pumps through several large, open tanks along one wall. These tanks hold Harbor Fish Market's live lobsters in a "pound" full of circulating sea water that's pumped right in from below the market. The tanks hold lobsters that have been weighed and sorted, from the smallest one-pound "chix" to one-and-three-quarter-pound "jumbos." Upon receiving a customer's order, a staff member will fish out a lobster from the appropriate tank with a large green mesh dip net.

Harbor Fish Market's practices are inspired by traditional fishmongers and lobster pounds, the first of which was developed on Vinalhaven in 1875. But the forty-five-year-old family-owned business has had to adapt its practices to the constant demands of the seafood world. The Alfiero family has vowed that they "won't sell anything they won't bring home themselves,"[172] and in doing so, they have garnered legions of loyal customers.

Customers' trust in the Alfiero family's products comes from the business's mission to serve fresh, high-quality seafood. Their seafood is never soaked, bleached or gassed (unethical practices used to extend the appearance of freshness) and is always sold fresh, unless it's clearly labeled as previously frozen. While Harbor Fish Market employees source seafood from all over the world, they are constantly researching what is sustainable and responsible to sell. For example, while it's legal to sell shark and Chilean sea bass, Harbor Fish has made the decision not to because of the danger of overfishing.[173]

The staff at Harbor Fish Market are always good for a recipe or preparation recommendation—the Alfiero family recently published a cookbook detailing their favorite recipes. Nick Alfiero recommends slightly undercooking seafood, since "overcooking is really the only way to

The no-frills exterior of Harbor Fish Market on Portland's Custom House Wharf. *Photo by Kate McCarty.*

totally botch it."[174] While many think of simply steaming lobsters, Alfiero recommends many methods of preparation that go well beyond. His lobster shortcake is a classic New England recipe of lobster tail and claw meat served with a sherry cream sauce over homemade biscuits. More ambitious home cooks might tackle Alfiero's baked stuffed lobster, which, lest you think it sounds too fancy, includes crushed Ritz crackers in the stuffing.

Until this year, Harbor Fish Market was one of the best places in Portland to get the freshest Maine shrimp. These tiny pink shrimp are native to the North Atlantic Ocean, including the Gulf of Maine, and are caught in January and February. They're available whole or "head-on" at Harbor Fish Market after the shrimping fleet sells its catch at the morning's fish auction. But for the first time in thirty-five years, the Atlantic States Marine Fisheries Commission declared that there would be no shrimping season in 2014.

During the 2014 moratorium, Harbor Fish Market briefly carried Northern shrimp caught in Canadian waters. Canadian shrimp stocks are thought to be increasing as the shrimp travel north to avoid the warming waters in the south. Portlanders looking forward to this sweet midwinter treat savored others like scallops and smelts, also only available in the winter.

The issue of seafood sustainability is ever-changing, and the Alfiero family and their staff work hard to keep up with the latest requirements.

Harbor Fish Market's air freight department is popular with out-of-staters who want a taste of Maine lobster. The lobsters are packed with seaweed and shipped live, to arrive within twenty-four to thirty-six hours. The Alfiero family has been in business long enough to see the development of these air freight routes and, with them, the stabilization of lobster prices. With the help of FedEx, Harbor Fish Market pioneered live lobster shipping in the early '80s, whereas before that, Alfiero remembers, "It was a rare and expensive treat to enjoy Maine lobsters anywhere but in Maine."[175]

Fortunately, visitors and locals can readily enjoy the freshest seafood from Maine and around the world from Portland's seafood markets like Harbor Fish Market and Browne Trading Company. Harbor Fish Market may be the perennial favorite of many Portlanders, with Browne Trading Company seen as the shop for a special occasion. These two anchors of Portland's working waterfront have shaped the seafood industry with their innovative seafood shipping methods. Yet traditional methods of seafood preservation are still used, like Browne Trading's smoking program and Harbor Fish's lobster pounds. While the two markets provide different experiences for their customers, both have the freshest seafood and a dedication to quality in common.

Chapter 12

EATING LOCALLY YEAR ROUND AT THE FARMERS' MARKET

A city's farmers' market is a good indicator of how connected the city remains to its local food system. Some markets may include fruits and vegetables from far-away states, while others may be a mix of crafts, prepared foods and produce vendors. In Portland, the farmers' market is mandated by city regulation that everything sold must be produced in the state of Maine. Vendors must also produce 75 percent of what they sell, which means the value-added products like honey, cider and preserves are local as well.[176] As a result, Portland's farmers' market is a fantastic showcase of the state's best meat, vegetables, fruit, honey, syrup, plants and baked and canned goods.

A stroll through the market on a sunny summer day under the leaf cover of the tall oaks in Deering Oaks Park reveals a bounty of locally produced food. Olivia's Garden sells its hydroponic English cucumbers, butter lettuces and cocktail tomatoes. Jars of Thirty Acre Farm's lacto-fermented sauerkraut, hot sauce and pickles sit alongside a rainbow of radishes. The staff at Beckwith Gardens' stand have arranged green cardboard pint boxes full of small, sweet Maine blueberries into geometric patterns on a gingham tablecloth. Samples of Swallowtail Creamery's crumbly aged and fresh herbed cheeses attract a crowd.

In the summer, the farmers' market happens twice a week: on Wednesdays in Monument Square and on Saturdays in Deering Oaks Park. The market was established in 1768 and is one of the oldest continuously operating markets in the country. The farmers' market began in Monument Square in a public market house located where the monument stands now. The

The Portland Farmers' Market takes place weekly in Deering Oaks Park. Thirty Acre Farm offers a bounty of summer produce. *Photo by Kate McCarty.*

Cranberries and apples for sale at the Portland Farmers' Market in the fall. Many eagerly anticipate apple season in Maine, where hundreds of varieties are grown. *Photo by Kate McCarty.*

building was remodeled in 1832, and Portland City Hall moved in. The market was displaced and changed locations several times before finally settling on Federal Street.[177]

In 1990, the Porteous department store closed (where the Maine College of Art is now), causing city officials to fear a declining downtown. The Farmers' Market Association relocated the market to Monument Square in an attempt to revitalize the area. At the same time, the Saturday market moved from a less frequented side of Deering Oaks Park to its current home on Farmers' Market Way.

Today, with more than thirty vendors in the summer, the Portland Farmers' Market is a bustling scene of local food, art, craft and live music. As the demand for local food increases, the farmers' market has become more and more popular for vendors and shoppers alike. Farmer and market membership coordinator Carolyn Snell says, "Customer demand is high for quality vegetables and quality food in general. People really want to know the story of their food, and the farmers' market is a great way for them to do that."[178]

The Snell Family Farm of Buxton has been a vendor at the Portland Farmers' Market since 1980, when Carolyn's parents, John and Ramona, expanded their family's orchard to include a greenhouse and a large vegetable garden. Now Carolyn works at the farm, too, and has her own business selling the farm's cut flowers and arrangements. Snell has seen the Wednesday market relocated from its Federal Street location to Monument Square and witnessed the founding of a thriving winter market.[179]

Snell is happy with how much the market has grown over the years. She says, "We feel that we're part of the community. We're happy that customers are here." But she is realistic about people's purchasing habits: "Our goal is not necessarily for everyone to get every single thing they could ever possibly want from us. We just want to see them every week. Or even once a month is great."[180]

The Portland Winter Farmers' Market is in its third year and in its best location yet. At 200 Anderson Street in East Bayside, the weekly Saturday market shares a space with a food production hub. Urban Farm Fermentory founder Eli Cayer has worked to rezone and renovate a large warehouse that houses his business and several other food producers. Formerly a taxi garage, the food hub is shared by two bakeries, a gourmet popsicle maker, a creamery and Cayer's fermentory.

The Portland Farmers' Market Association saw the newly renovated space in East Bayside as the perfect place to host the indoor winter farmers' market.

"That part of town is such a hotbed right now," says Snell.[181] The food hub's businesses continue to attract customers through the spring, even though the market's produce selection dwindles midwinter. The winter market in its new location has been extremely successful compared to past years.

In an effort to help more people buy local foods, the farmers' market association implemented a program to enable customers to use debit, credit and SNAP (food stamps) cards. Typically, farmers' market vendors don't accept these methods of payment because of the additional cost of a processing machine. To solve that problem, the market established a token program in 2011 with funds from nonprofit Cultivating Community.[182] Customers can pay for wooden tokens at a booth and then use the tokens to purchase fresh food from any market vendor. The vendors are then reimbursed by the market for their sales. As a result of this program, Maine boasts the second-largest amount of total food stamp dollars spent on local foods in the country.[183]

No matter how people are buying local food, they're doing it in droves year round at the Portland Farmers' Market. In a town with myriad local food purchasing options, the market still reigns supreme as the place to connect with local farmers.

Chapter 13

CUTTING IN THE MIDDLEMAN

The Brighton Avenue location of Rosemont Market & Bakery sits on the corner of a busy intersection in the suburbs of Portland. The store is small but hard to miss due to its brightly colored exterior and chalkboard sandwich sign that during this particular week proclaims, "Get psyched for apples!" Inside, stacked wooden crates are filled with local produce: ears of late-season corn with crackly husks, striped dark-green winter squash, hardneck garlic, greenhouse tomatoes and more colors and shapes of potatoes than I've ever seen in one place before.

Refrigerator coolers are stocked with local dairy products and prepared foods that are made in-house. A cabinet full of breads and sweets stands next to an expansive but affordable wine section. In the back, staff work behind deli counters full of local meat and cheeses, ready to help with a recommendation or prepare a custom cut. The store is full of shoppers, some in for a cup of coffee and a cookie and others picking up a basket of fresh ingredients for dinner. Rosemont Market is part farmers' market, part deli and part gourmet shop. Not everything sold at the market is local, but it is sourced locally whenever possible. Rather, the store's motto is, "Not more than you need, just exactly what you want—and the best of it."[184] The store is like a European-style market, where people shop three to four times a week for fresh ingredients.

Store owner John Naylor started the Rosemont Market with baker Scott Anderson after the two worked together at the now defunct Portland Greengrocer. The relationships Naylor formed at the Greengrocer helped

Bins of local produce for sale at Rosemont Market & Bakery. *Photo by Kate McCarty.*

him stock his new store. Manager Joe Appel explains, "From the very beginning it was based on our relationships that John had with farmers, and our chicken guy, and our dairy people, before 'locavore' was a word. It's just what we did. We were selling food from around here."[185] The surprisingly simple model has been well received in Portland, where the market has expanded to two additional locations, with a fourth in Yarmouth.

Between the knowledgeable staff and their small but high-quality inventory, Rosemont Market feels refreshingly sincere. You can tell that the people who work here care about food. "The guys who work in the butcher department were chefs at Fore Street for three years," says Appel. "But you don't have the relationships you can form with customers when you're in the back of the house in a restaurant. And so here, you do, and that's what has drawn so many people here." Whether as employees or shoppers, people are attracted to Rosemont Market for the close connections between food and community.[186]

Organic or conventional. Local or from away. Everything is well labeled at the store, and store employees are on hand to provide additional information. Of course, you can pop in and out of the market without having to hear the history of your food. But should you want to know where your vegetables come from, Rosemont employees are happy to tell you. Providing a valuable link to local foods, Rosemont Market continues to shorten the distance between people and the source of their food. In doing so, it has built a community of butchers, bakers, farmers and caring consumers.

Martha Putnam of the local foods distribution company Farm Fresh Connection says that Rosemont Market is her number-one customer. She says, "I want to make a big blue ribbon for them to put on their wall that says, 'Number One Buyer of Local Produce.'"[187] Putnam sources local produce from local farmers and sells it to local businesses like restaurants, schools and Sysco distributors. Rosemont's Appel says that Putnam is a crucial link between farmers and points of sale like his market.[188]

Putnam founded her business after getting her start in the first iteration of the Portland Public Market House in 1999. The market's management hired her to coordinate the two local produce stands. This work connected her with farmers and local producers all over the state. Then in her early twenties, she laughs as she remembers being approached by the Maine Sustainable Agriculture Society (MSAS), a nonprofit dedicated to improving and promoting the state's sustainable agriculture.[189] "They thought I was an expert at 'local,'" Putnam says.[190] (And she may very well have been. If she wasn't then, she is now.)

Rosemont Market & Bakery supports local farmers and producers with its wide selection of local and organic produce. *Photo by Kate McCarty.*

Maine Sustainable Agriculture Society asked Putnam to write a proposal for a business that would distribute local foods to institutions like hospitals and schools. The Sustainable Agricultural Society saw midsized farms going out of business due to high costs of distribution. Smaller grocery stores were being bought out by supermarkets and Walmart, making it a challenge for certain farms to supply the larger orders required by bigger businesses. With the decreasing number of midsize farms, the state was not only losing farmland but also the ability to grow food.[191]

Putnam's plan for a local foods distribution company was then to connect with farmers who are good at growing vegetables but don't have the time or money to distribute their products. Farm Fresh Connection was approved by MSAS, with support from Maine Organic Farmers and Gardeners Association (MOFGA), and funded by a grant from Common Good Ventures. Putnam purchased the business from MSAS after the grant funding ended. Despite the fact that her actual operations turned out nothing like her proposed plan, fifteen years later Putnam's business represents one hundred Maine growers and does more than $1 million in sales per year.[192]

Putnam's farm stand at her husband's family farm, Wealden Farm, in Freeport is stocked with an amazing variety of local products. Midwinter,

Putnam is selling vine-ripened tomatoes from Backyard Farms in Madison. The cooler is full of Hahn's End cheese from Debbie Hahn in Phippsburg. There's gallons of maple syrup, two-pound bags of dried beans, quarts of honey and bushels of winter squash and Macintosh apples. If you think eating locally in Maine is only a seasonal affair, you'd do well to visit Putnam's farm stand and see the variety.

Farm Fresh Connection and Rosemont Market are but two ways in which Mainers access their locally grown food. Both, in the words of Joe Appel, "knit more closely together the community of producers, makers, restaurants and chefs and avid amateurs."[193] In providing a place for these community members to come together, the two businesses continue to strengthen Maine's regional food system.

Chapter 14
LOCAL VENDORS WITH
A BIG MISSION

When you first enter the Public Market House on Portland's Monument Square, you'll find yourself right in the middle of a bustling scene. The two main doors open into a narrow aisle bordered by stalls displaying cheese, fruits, vegetables and freshly baked pizzas and breads. If you pause for a moment to take in your surroundings, customers on their lunch break will squeeze by you on their way upstairs for a cup of soup, a burrito or a coffee.

This is not to say that one can't linger comfortably in the market. The staff at the gourmet shop are happy to share samples from their extensive selection of European and domestic cheeses. The beer and wine shop in the back may be hosting a wine tasting where a knowledgeable employee will tell you about their handpicked selection. Make your way upstairs, and you'll find a food court with five shops, big windows, tall ceilings and plenty of seating at small tables and couches.

The two-story Public Market House is a conglomeration of small food and drink businesses that on the surface looks like a nice place to have lunch or pick up a bottle of wine. But talk to market founder Kris Horton, and you'll quickly realize that the mission of the market is much loftier than turning a profit. Horton is the proprietor of K. Horton's Specialty Foods, a shop on the first floor that will draw you in with its large cases of cheese, olives, smoked seafood and spreads.

Together with Bill Milliken and Andrew Braceras of Maine Beer and Beverage Co., Horton started the current iteration of the Portland Public Market in 2006. The two businesses began in the original Public Market House,

Kris Horton in her Portland Public Market House shop. Horton helped to start the Public Market and supports many local businesses in her work. *Photo by Kate McCarty.*

located on Cumberland Avenue, a few blocks away from its current location. The philanthropic Libra Foundation opened the Portland Public Market House in 1998 in an effort to reverse the decline of Portland's downtown area.[194]

The newly constructed, thirty-seven-thousand-square-foot timber-framed space housed twenty-eight vendors, including K. Horton's, Maine Beer and Beverage Co. and Big Sky Bakery, plus farm stands, a florist and two restaurants: The Commissary and Scales. The Commissary was a fine dining restaurant from chef Matthew Kenney, a Maine chef who now owns four restaurants across the country, including the Gothic in Belfast. Scales was a retail and prepared seafood market owned by Dana Street of Street & Co. and Fore Street.[195] The Public Market House was a beautiful, lavish celebration of local foods that was ultimately hindered by differing views of success between market management and its tenants. The Libra Foundation closed the market in 2006, citing failure to make a profit.

When the original Public Market closed, Horton and two other businesses decided to band together to purchase a new building in which to continue the market. Horton explains:

In order to advocate the goals of a public market, we really needed to commit to a lot more space than we needed for ourselves. And that was pretty scary. As three small business owners, we took on the commitment of three times the space that we needed. And that was just in the hopes that someone else would come along and want to start a business with us.[196]

Now in their seventh year of business, Horton has found that plenty of businesses want to be a part of the Public Market's model.

The market's prime location on Monument Square provides an easy way for small businesses to reach customers. "Part of our formula for how to succeed was to have other businesses subleasing from us," says Horton. By providing space for five businesses on the second floor, the Public Market House decreases the overhead needed for a new business to acquire a retail space. Some businesses are so successful that they graduate from the market, going on to acquire their own space.[197]

What makes the Public Market House more than a typical market is the shared resources it provides small businesses. A commercial kitchen in the basement of the Public Market is available to rent by the hour. This space allows people to produce value-added food products for sale without licensing their own kitchens, often a costly hurdle. Local Sprouts Cooperative's catering operation used the space for two years before opening a café in its own space. The Public Market also pays the city for sidewalk space and then rents day tables to very small businesses. Frequently farmers, bakers and craft vendors set up tables during the Wednesday farmers' market. These tables further extend the mission of the market as an incubator for small businesses.[198]

Most of the vendors in the market feature Maine-made products, most notably in Kris Horton's shop. Horton sells the biggest selection of Maine cheeses, sometimes being the only retail outlet other than the local farmers' market where a certain cheese is available. Horton acknowledges that "[i]t takes a personality running that business that's willing to take on small producers. But the Public Market will always be an outlet for businesses to get started and for people to sell their products. So we do a lot more than run a little shop," she laughs.[199]

Horton is helping small Maine-based food businesses by selling their products and allowing them to concentrate on the production. The closing of the first Public Market allowed Horton to see how a division of labor between the producers and the retailers could be beneficial. "In the farm world and the cheese world, a lot of businesses don't want to get really big," she says. "They like the quality of their life as much as they like their product."[200]

In asking farmers to keep retail hours in the Public Market, many were struggling with the time commitment. In fact, Horton's father was one who benefited from having her act as his retail proxy. He produced smoked seafood and had previously been selling only wholesale to accounts across the country, including American Airlines. When Horton began selling his smoked seafood at the Public Market, it was the first time anyone in Portland was able to buy his products retail. "He was a model of what the Public Market wants: somebody with really fine Maine product getting into the middle of the city," says Horton.[201]

Today, Horton and her business partners have found a way for the Public Market to fulfill its ideals of supporting small Maine businesses in a sustainable way. Just like so many other fantastic food businesses in Portland, this is one great place to get delicious, high-quality food while supporting the local food economy in many unseen ways.

Lobstermen unload their catch on Custom House Wharf, one of many that make up Portland's working waterfront. *Photo by Kate McCarty.*

Dean's Sweets' salted caramel truffles are handcrafted in the owners' Old Port shop. *Photo by Kate McCarty.*

East End Cupcakes' chocolate cakes with Italian buttercream frosting are a classic flavor combination. *Photo by Kate McCarty.*

Eventide Oyster Co.'s take on a lobster roll includes brown butter and a steamed bun. *Photo by Kate McCarty.*

Eventide Oyster Co. offers twenty oyster varieties from Maine and "from away." *Photo by Kate McCarty.*

Maine has the fastest-growing number of artisan cheesemakers, as evidenced by the wide selection of Maine cheeses sold by Kris Horton in her Portland Public Market House shop. *Photo by Kate McCarty.*

Nonesuch Oyster employees harvest and sort oysters from their skiff. Nonesuch oysters are grown in bags in the Scarborough River and are known for their sweet, grassy taste. *Photo by Kate McCarty.*

Beets from Fishbowl Farms for sale at the Portland Farmers' Market. *Photo by Phil Jellen.*

A course of foie gras and brown bread from Chef Rob Evans and Josh Potocki at the popular brunch series Pocket Brunch. *Photo by Kate McCarty.*

Bangs Island Mussels are served simply at Fore Street, steamed with almond butter and Standard Baking Co. bread for dipping. *Photo by Kate McCarty.*

Pork belly buns at Pai Men Miyake, the casual noodle bar from Japanese chef Masa Miyake. *Photo by Kate McCarty.*

A wide variety of local products is available for sale through Farm Fresh Connection's farm stand, including winter squash and hydroponically grown tomatoes. *Photo by Kate McCarty.*

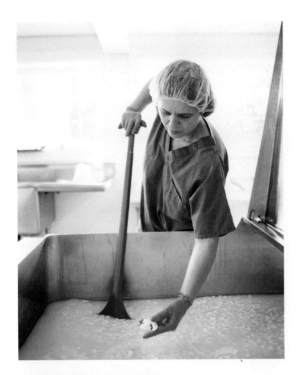

Top: Silvery Moon cheesemaker Dorothee Grimm stirs cheddar cheese curds at Smiling Hill Farm. *Photo by Greta Rybus.*

Left: Lucky Catch Lobster Tours captain Dave Lalibertie hauls traps aboard his boat in Casco Bay. *Photo by Greta Rybus.*

Top: About 90 percent of North American lobster is caught in Maine waters. No visit to Maine is complete without a taste of this delicacy. *Photo by Greta Rybus.*

Left: Portland chefs and markets purchase locally grown produce from Cape Elizabeth farmer Penny Jordan, who is known in particular for her beautiful lettuces. *Photo by Greta Rybus.*

Bins of cherry tomatoes for sale in the height of the summer at Jordan's Farm retail farm stand. *Photo by Greta Rybus.*

Miyake restaurants are known for their fresh seafood and creative Japanese fare, with a focus on sustainably sourced local ingredients. *Photo by Kate McCarty.*

Above: Browne Trading Company's smoked salmon and trout are smoked in-house with recipes inspired by traditional Midcoast Maine smoking methods. *Photo by Kate McCarty.*

Left: Tai snapper on ice at Browne Trading Company waiting to be processed and shipped to some of the finest seafood restaurants in the country. *Photo by Kate McCarty.*

Left: Cape Elizabeth's scenic Portland Head Light marks the entrance to Casco Bay. The park offers one of the most scenic dining spots in the Greater Portland area. *Photo by Greta Rybus.*

Below: Scenic pedestrian-only Wharf Street in Portland's Old Port offers myriad dining options. *Photo by Corey Templeton.*

Farmer Steve Burger milks a heritage breed Randall cow at Winter Hill Farm in Freeport. *Photo by Claire Houston.*

Salvage BBQ & Smokehouse offers barbecue classics like ribs, pulled pork sandwiches and hushpuppies. *Photo by Kate McCarty.*

Top: Lobster shacks like Sprague's in Wiscasset dot Maine's coast offering classic New England fare. *Photo by Greta Rybus.*

Left: Portland's East End Community School students work with Cultivating Community staff in the school garden. *Photo by Greta Rybus.*

Top: The school garden at Portland's East End Community School is part of a larger effort by Portland Public Schools to increase the use of local foods in city schools. *Photo by Greta Rybus.*

Left: A beautiful grass-fed lamb dish from Emilitsa in Portland, a Greek restaurant that uses many local and organic ingredients. *Photo by Zack Bowen.*

Left: Duckfat is well known for its Belgian-style fries made from Maine potatoes and fried in duck fat. *Photo by Zack Bowen.*

Below: Dishes like this locally farmed venison are carefully constructed at Hugo's. *Photo by Zack Bowen.*

Chefs at Hugo's prep for dinner service in the restaurant's open kitchen, where the majority of the seating is at the bar, right in front of the action. *Photo by Zack Bowen.*

East Ender serves American fare with a creative twist, featuring local ingredients in a pub-style setting. *Photo by Zack Bowen.*

Chapter 15
FARM-TO-TRUCK DINING

Food trucks are a hallmark of a city's dining scene, and like most things, it took a while for them to arrive in Portland. The problem wasn't ever a lack of enthusiasm for street food. The city had a flourishing food cart scene—Mark of Mark's Hotdogs has been dutifully serving his cart's fare in the Old Port for more than thirty years. Rather, the problem stemmed from a rather arbitrary cart size restriction.

Until mid-2012, the city's regulations only allowed small mobile food carts. Most food carts sell lunch in the Old Port and on Commercial Street, but a few dedicated folks wanted more opportunity and were willing to work to change the rules. After a year of bureaucratic effort, food trucks were allowed limited operation in certain spots in Portland. Within the burgeoning fleet of eight food trucks, many food truckers believe that the current regulations still need improving in order for the movement to really take off.

Inspired by the thriving mobile dining scene after a visit to Austin, Texas, husband and wife Karl and Sarah Sutton began looking into starting a food truck in Portland. They quickly discovered that the current city rules and regulations didn't allow for mobile food vending from large trucks or trailers. In their research, however, they found that Fort Williams in Cape Elizabeth, the park that surrounds the iconic Portland Head Light and reportedly receives more than 1 million visitors per year, was accepting applications for the first food vendors in the park.[202] The Suttons began pursuing a location in the park instead of Portland and were ultimately accepted.

In researching bringing food trucks to Portland, the Suttons connected with Ron Gan, a Portland realtor who was looking into opening a barbecue food truck. Together, the three approached Andy Graham, a board member of the nonprofit Creative Portland, where Graham works to promote Portland as an attractive place for creative people.[203] Graham saw the food truck issue as one of economic, creative and entrepreneurial development. Eventually, the city formed a food truck task force, composed of Graham, city council members, the Portland Downtown District and restaurant representatives. The task force crafted a set of recommendations for food trucks that the city passed in the winter of 2012.[204]

While diners celebrated the impending mobile food revolution, it became apparent to potential business owners that the regulations passed by the city were too restrictive for food trucks to thrive. Sarah Sutton recalls Ron Gan warning the city that "they would be surprised there aren't a lot of people willing to open trucks under these circumstances."[205]

Many felt that the areas and hours in which food trucks were allowed to operate weren't expansive enough to allow an opportunity for financial success. The geographic restrictions were the task force's attempt at protecting the brick-and-mortar restaurants from the loss of business should a food truck be in proximity. Food trucks are only allowed on the outermost reaches of the Portland peninsula, away from the tourist- and pedestrian-heavy areas of the Old Port.

Food truck hopefuls were further dismayed that many of the less contentious recommendations from the task force didn't make it into legislation at all. Food trucks weren't allowed to cluster together, a common food truck practice that helps to attract more diners. After countless hours spent e-mailing and discussing the mistakes, the Suttons helped to convince the city to revise the regulations to allow food truck clustering. Clustering was added to the city's regulations late in the summer of 2013. But Karl and Sarah feel that the existing regulations still don't go far enough to allow food trucks to thrive. "There's a very stringent ordinance in existence in terms of long-term success for people. There's opportunities for [the city] to expand it even further," says Sarah.[206]

For their part, the Suttons have remained committed to helping to revise the Portland food truck regulations, even though they operate their business in Cape Elizabeth. They currently serve lobster rolls at Fort Williams Park from their seventy-two-square-foot cart. Sarah's enthusiasm for her work and food carts in general is apparent.

The Suttons serve six iterations of lobster rolls: Maine-style (chilled, with mayonnaise), Connecticut-style (warm, tossed with butter), picnic-style

The Bite Into Maine food cart sells classic and creative lobster rolls and other Maine classics in Cape Elizabeth's scenic Fort Williams Park. *Photo by Greta Rybus.*

(with coleslaw), curry, wasabi and chipotle, all on grilled split-top buns. The Suttons are meticulous about their ingredients, using fresh, never frozen lobster meat, which is a more difficult feat than you might imagine. Once while I was lunching at the cart, Karl very intently asked me my opinion of the bread, since they'd recently switched suppliers.

The colorful Bite Into Maine trailer is towed to and from the park every day of the summer season, and for the first time, the Suttons operated at Sunday River Ski Resort for the winter months this year. After three seasons, Karl sees their business steadily improving. "After our first season, it was kind of rough," he says. "The next year got a lot better since people were familiar with us, and our sales got a lot better. It's like any kind of business: in the first season, you're building up a following."[207]

Food truckers Karl Deuben and Bill Leavy of Small Axe knew that navigating business in the winter would be the hardest part of their new endeavor. The two chefs decided to open a food truck after working together for years in the kitchens of some of Portland's finest restaurants. "We became good friends at Hugo's," says Leavy. "I'd always follow Karl [to a restaurant], and then he would leave and I'd be stuck there without him," he laughs. "And I'm still following him now—he talked me into this food truck."[208]

Initially looking to open their own restaurant, the chef duo decided on a truck, attracted to the versatility and low overhead of a mobile kitchen.

However, Leavy says, "It's challenging. You take a lot of things for granted in a brick-and-mortar restaurant," like gas, water and electricity. "We work ten- to twelve-hour days and still look at what needs to be prepped for the next day."[209]

After their first season, their bright orange truck is extremely popular, the aim of which, according to Deuben, is to serve "carefully crafted food that tastes good."[210] Their small, distinct menu uses locally sourced and sometimes unusual ingredients like the Shishito peppers on their Lightning Smokestack burger—a cold-smoked beef patty with Jack cheese, those spicy peppers and Gochujang ketchup on a soft 158 Pickett Street Café bun. The burger was a hit with diners but was only on the menu while the Shishito peppers were available. "That burger was made for those peppers," says Deuben.[211] When the peppers went out of season, the burger was replaced by the equally popular Pineapple Express, a smoked and braised beef brisket sandwich topped with pineapple relish and fried onion rings.

The chefs use organic vegetables from Green Spark Farm in Cape Elizabeth and get their fish from Salt + Sea Community Supported Fishery. They developed their relationships with these local purveyors while working at Hugo's and Miyake. Deuben would shop for vegetables for the sushi restaurant's omakase at the farmers' market. Here, he noticed the unusual varieties of vegetables that Mary Ellen and Austin Chadd grow at their farm. In starting their own business, Deuben and Leavy felt that it was important to continue to support these small producers.[212]

While Small Axe food truck moves around a bit, their favorite location is on the Tandem Coffee Roasters and Bunker Brewing Co. "campus" in Portland's East Bayside neighborhood. Originally, Deuben and Leavy partnered with the roaster and brewery because they figured that the two businesses would attract a steady crowd of locals. They found, however, that because this industrial neighborhood has received its fair share of press, it has become a tourist attraction in its own right.

The neighborhood is home to two breweries, a fermentory, a winery, two coffee roasters and newly expanded food production spaces. Deuben embraces the entrepreneurial spirit that these new businesses share in this up-and-coming neighborhood. "I like being on the outskirts," he says. Leavy agrees, adding, "Bayside has been really great to us; we love being down here. It's a good community crowd, and they seem to like what we do. [Small Axe] fits well with craft beer and craft coffee."[213] The strong culinary background and community connections of the chefs behind Small Axe truck will guarantee their continued success.

The Small Axe food truck is frequently parked outside the Bunker Brewing Co. in Portland's East Bayside neighborhood. *Photo by Anestes Fotiades.*

What Sarah Sutton hopes for the future of the food truck movement in Portland is that the city's regulations evolve so others can be successful too. She'd like to see designated city parking spots for food trucks and fewer restrictions on operating hours and locations: "We've talked a lot about having a place in the city designated to food trucks where they're permitted, they have access to electricity, they're set up for the season. It's like a food truck food court. And what if all the city parks were open to food trucks? They could make a schedule; they could cluster there. The city parks are open and encouraging people to come because there's food there."

Currently, food vendors in city parks operate using a bidding process that allows one truck or cart per park. In the summer of 2012, only one food truck and one cart took advantage of the ability to serve food in the city's parks.[214]

Karl Sutton believes that the proper set of regulations would balance restaurants' and mobile food vendors' needs. "We don't believe in a total free-for-all. I just don't think it has to be so adversarial," he says. "It would be nice to see a supportive environment, to see it as part of the puzzle for Portland, [with the city saying,] 'How can we support this in a smart way?'"[215] The Suttons continue to make recommendations to the city council on behalf of the Portland food truck owners, hoping to see a comprehensive set of ordinances that will allow the mobile dining scene to flourish.

Chapter 16
PORTLAND POP-UPS

What we love about pop-up meals may ultimately be what causes them to end. To the diner, these meals are spontaneous, unpredictable, secretive and extravagant. To the staff, they're all of those things, plus a lot of work. A reoccurring series perhaps even becomes hindered by the public's expectations. But in a community full of talented kitchen professionals, these fleeting dining experiences are relished by cooks and diners alike.

In Portland, several pop-up dining events came and went recently. Some transformed into permanent restaurants, and others dissolved but hopefully will appear again. Two chefs from Local 188 hosted Cloak + Dagger, a themed dinner pop-up series; the final meal moved to New York and then disbanded. Sonnet, Damian Sansonetti's series, ended so he could focus on opening his restaurant, Piccolo. We previewed Vinland, David Levi's 100 percent local foods restaurant, at the Hush, Hush event, a cocktail party collaboration with the Portland Hunt & Alpine Club.

The longest-running pop-up series was Pocket Brunch, a monthly themed brunch series. The product of a group of talented chefs, restaurant owners and bartenders, the events were exceedingly popular, with tickets frequently selling out in just a few hours.

The first Pocket Brunch was held at Joel Beauchamp's house, with Beauchamp, Josh Potocki of 158 Pickett Street Café and guest chef Rocco Salvatore Talarico cooking. After five courses, including buttermilk-fried frog legs and rosettes with walnut panna cotta, happy diners urged the chefs and organizers to continue the series. "It was unbelievable to see the outpouring of support from the community, the way it started to roll. We ended up having to choose between venues rather than to try and find one," says Katie Schier-Potocki of the Bread and Butter Catering Company, who manages the events.[216]

Over the course of a year, Pocket Brunch became one of the most popular dining events in Portland. In addition to the talent of the organizers, a guest chef was invited, featuring chefs from Portland restaurants including Miyake, Fore Street and Duckfat.[217]

The themes for the monthly brunches evolved out of the location or the featured chef; Chef Nate Nadeau of Fore Street welcomed the opportunity to cook some of his native French Canadian cuisine. Chef Karl Deuben's "Farm Hands" meal included a course of toasted hay–infused soup and gingerbread in terra-cotta flower pots for dessert at Broadturn Farm. "Each chef that was onboard got to show their stuff, but outside of their box that they're always stuck in," says event bartender Nan'l Meiklejohn.[218]

The only Pocket Brunch I attended was in January, dubbed "Baller Brunch" with Chef Rob Evans. The daylong event was held at Broadturn Farm, which was transformed into a winter wonderland with pine boughs, milk glass and festive paper poofs hanging in the barn rafters. The meal itself was served in the greenhouse, set with communal tables covered in white linens. Spider plants and succulents perched over our tables on hanging shelves. Farmer Stacy Bliss said that she's always dreamed of a greenhouse restaurant, and she pulled it off for a day.[219]

In the farmhouse kitchen, Evans and Potocki served food that was both "balled" and "baller." The salad course was spicy gravlax, trout roe, a round of fried Maine potato shreds, crème fraîche and pistachio marmalade. The baller came out with the next course of twenty-three-carat gold-flaked foie gras, with apple butter, pickled apples, quince and brown bread. The meal lasted six hours and by the end resembled any farm party, with fire pits and groups of raucous smokers.

The brunches' pervasive theme always created an atmosphere that drew people looking for a unique dining experience. "What we were doing was attracting the people we wanted to feed," says Meiklejohn. "If you don't like not knowing where it's going to be until two days before, if you don't like not knowing what the menu is, it's not for you."[220] The crowds were always a mix of young and old, locals and visitors, industry people and food enthusiasts.

Ultimately, even the self-imposed expectations of Pocket Brunch began to feel too restrictive for the organizers. While a final Pocket Brunch with the chefs of Hugo's has been hinted at, they've taken a yearlong hiatus. But, says

Guests await their first course at Pocket Brunch in Broadturn Farm's greenhouse. *Photo by Kate McCarty.*

Schier-Potocki, they're looking for new ways to continue their dining events. "I think taking a break has been good, since we have newfound motivation to see what happens next," she says.[221]

She and Meiklejohn are looking forward to continuing their dining series with different events in unlikely locations. Schier-Potocki has her eye on a schooner in Portland Harbor that, without a kitchen, isn't ideal for a Pocket Brunch. She is thinking that it's perfect for a cocktail party with passed appetizers. Meiklejohn hosted pop-up cocktail parties at SPACE Gallery that morphed into plans for his own bar, called the Jewel Box, one block away.[222]

Whatever the series evolves into, between their talent in the kitchen and the support of their community, the Pocket Brunch crew will be successful. "It was probably the greatest thing we could have done to prove we live in the right place, and [that] we love where we live," says Schier-Potocki.[223]

Chapter 17

SELLING LOCAL FOODS COOPERATIVELY

In a world of global corporations, sweatshop labor and overseas production, it feels refreshing to meet owners and employees of businesses who are happy to discuss their business models and product sources with you. After talking to several participants of two local food cooperatives, I get the impression that owners of cooperative businesses are thoughtful people. Rachelle Curran Apse, board member of the Portland Food Co-op, tells me that a co-op volunteer asked her if the board had thought of how local art will be displayed at their new retail store. Apse had not, so she was delighted to find that this woman was willing to lend her professional skills and coordinate with local artists.

Local Sprouts Cooperative employees Abby Huckel and Kelly Rioux describe how all of the products used at their café are carefully sourced, from the hot sauce to the chocolate to the waste-removal services. A map on the wall of Local Sprouts Cooperative Café is labeled with the locations of its forty-plus food and drink vendors.

These are the people enthusiastically thinking about the minute details of an otherwise mundane experience like grocery shopping and product orders. But in considering the details of their businesses, cooperatives are contributing to the community and the environment while providing a way for people to shop and eat that they can feel good about. These cooperative projects take more work, time and energy than the already demanding work of running a small business. But it's because of, not in spite of, these demands that cooperative businesses attract dedicated individuals who are willing to work hard to enrich their communities.

The Many Faces of the Portland Food Co-op

Fans of local food in Portland have always lamented the loss of the city's natural foods store. They point to the fantastic food co-ops in Belfast and Damariscotta and ask, "Why don't we have one?" The frequent answer is that, instead, there's Whole Foods Market, Trader Joe's and Hannaford. But since Whole Foods Market bought out the Whole Grocer in 2005, a group of individuals has been dedicated to the idea of opening a member-owned natural foods store.

Rachelle Curran Apse is one of the original organizers, and she says that when the Whole Grocer closed, "there was a lot of connection to this idea of the private, natural foods store being yours. And [when it closed,] people realized, 'Oh, it's not really ours.'"[224] The member-owned cooperative model was a way for the community to ensure the existence of their natural foods store.

Now, six years later, the Portland Food Co-op has announced its plans to open a retail store. Its leased space is in half of a languishing plaza on Congress Street in Portland's East End. The store will be renovated and built out to members' specifications. Apse and the other board members are particularly excited about the store's location. She says, "We recognized that you need good parking to be successful. But ideally, we're also in a community and we're on the peninsula. And the number of spots that have parking and [are] on the peninsula? We felt so lucky."[225]

While the retail store has been the food co-op's goal all along, members created an interim buying club while they built the necessary resources for the store. In 2008, the board's research into opening a retail store revealed that the process takes an average of five years. That felt like a really long time to some people.

So, to satisfy the more immediate need for local foods purchasing, the members started buying in bulk from local foods distributor Crown O' Maine and bulk organic products co-op Frontier. They used the Meg Perry Center, a community-driven cooperative space on Congress Street, to receive bulk orders and split cases of food into members' orders. Eventually, they outgrew the space and moved to their own store on Hampshire Street. The co-op's next move will hopefully be its last as it realizes its goal of operating a member-owned grocery store that's open to everyone.

The Portland Food Co-op's model is a fairly common one in the world of cooperatives. Every member contributes equity and, in turn, receives an equal share of the business. Member-owners then vote on policies and business decisions. Most recently, the co-op's board held a meeting to get input from member-owners about the design of the new retail store. All of the store's policies and overall vision will be created by the member-owners. Apse references the goal of a "triple bottom line," a common principle of cooperatives. "The goal is to be financially sustainable," she says, "and to make sure you're committed to the community and environmental sustainability."[226]

The buyers' club option will continue for member-owners until the retail store opens later this year. Apse acknowledges that the buyers' club model requires a lot of volunteer time and effort and, therefore, is not sustainable. She and the other board members are recruiting four times as many member-owners for the retail store as they had in the buyers' club. It's still a lot of work, but they're moving toward a more sustainable model. "I'm most inspired by a space for people to engage in a meaningful way in society," says Apse. "The engine is volunteers, and that's because people want to see this thriving community center where you get to go and buy all your groceries."[227]

An Evolving Conversation

Local Sprouts Cooperative is a worker-owned café that—on top of serving delicious food, local draft beer and its own baked goods—is a community space for art, music and education. Every facet of the business is carefully decided by the member-owners, who are guided by a shared set of values. Locally produced food takes center stage at the café, but their work in supporting the local food economy is also woven throughout the café's community programs with nonprofits like Cultivating Community and public in-store educational workshops.

The thoughtful way in which the worker-owners of Local Sprouts Cooperative do business is most apparent on the café's menu. The café serves a wide variety of dishes, from a vegan BLT sandwich made with tempeh bacon to traditional French Canadian buckwheat ployes served with Maine maple syrup. But Local Sprouts also serves a cheeseburger made with grass-fed ground beef and organic chicken tenders with potato wedges. Member-owner Abby Huckel says that she's trying to promote the café as having a "great menu...where everybody can be satisfied and not have to compromise on what they order."[228]

Kelly Rioux estimates that about 80 percent of their food is locally sourced and cites the additional amount of work this requires. The café

At Local Sprouts Cooperative Café, employees work hard to source 80 percent of their products locally. *Photo by Kate McCarty.*

has more than forty food vendors, compared to the handful of distributors from which another restaurant might buy. But the worker-owners find the additional labor involved with coordinating these local food producers to be worthwhile. Huckel says, "One of the most gratifying parts of being a part of this business is all these relationships we have. There are all these cool people in Maine growing food or producing food products that we can have a relationship with." Huckel would much rather know the café's vendors than have the ease of purchasing from one food distribution company.

Rioux also says that she finds her work at Local Sprouts Café extremely gratifying. Rioux has been a worker-owner since the café opened in 2010. "You feel like you have your values in line with the place that you work," she says. "It's a lot of work…you put the time in, but your voice is absolutely heard."[229] Rioux frequently mentions the ongoing conversation about business practices among the worker-owners.

Discussing a company field trip to EcoMaine, the recycling and waste management facility, Rioux says, "There's a lot that goes into the local food industry that's so much more than [daily operations]. It's great to get outside and see…this is the waste we're producing by being a business. We have a lot of conversations about that. And because we're a democratic restaurant… we talk about these things. If someone has a concern, we talk about it."[230]

Rioux and Huckel's frequent mentions of conversations and talking make me wonder about the efficiency of a cooperative business model. With more than twenty café worker-owners, it takes a lot of time and energy to get everyone's opinion about brands of hot sauce, for example. The café does have position specializations, like the newly hired purchasing coordinator who is responsible for overseeing the many food vendors that supply the café.

Ultimately, though, the member-owners are not motivated by efficiency but rather by ensuring that their daily work is dedicated to a positive contribution to their community and its food. For her part, Apse acknowledges that a cooperative business model like the Portland Food Co-op is "a lot of work to get it up and going." But, she adds, "Once it's going, there's so many that are successful. They are a great model and a way for people to be more involved in their community and [to] know the story of their food. It's a true community project to start up."[231] While both businesses are relatively young, one thing that is for certain is the dedication of its owners. Now that the café and the food co-op retail store are established, Portland has that many more ways to support the local foods community.

Chapter 18
FOOD INSECURITY RELIEF

With so many people working to create good food in Portland, whether in their community garden or their restaurant kitchen, it's impossible to ignore that there are hungry people in our city. Preble Street Resource Center, a social services organization, estimates that five thousand Portland households depend on food pantry services every month.[232] Seniors on fixed incomes are particularly vulnerable to food insecurity, and Maine has the oldest population in the country.[233] Fortunately, there are many organizations and individuals dedicated to alleviating hunger by increasing people's access to food.

One is Stephanie Aquilina, who manages the food access projects at Cultivating Community. She's particularly excited about a new project for this summer. "The Grow Cart [is] a tricycle-powered mobile farm stand," she says. "We want to use that to deliver [Senior Farm] shares to different housing sites. The cart will allow us to bike up the produce very easily and then set up outside so there's a little farm stand."[234] The project is in collaboration with the organization's longtime volunteer Hannah Merchant, a recent Maine College of Art graduate. The Grow Cart is but one way that Cultivating Community is looking to bring local, affordable produce to Portland residents.[235]

Cultivating Community is a nonprofit that works to strengthen communities through food programs.[236] Its programs encompass a dizzying array of audiences and projects, but they all focus on food. The organization's offices are located in a small duplex in Portland's Kennedy Park public housing

Cultivating Community offers a variety of educational programs for new Mainers and kids, offering hands-on experience in the garden and the kitchen, as well as on the farm. *Photo by Greta Rybus.*

development. Cultivating Community's youth programs are hosted on its urban farm a few blocks away. The teenagers in the Community Culinary Crew cook spiced squash muffins in the office's kitchen, and the youth growers sell pints of snap peas and strawberries from a farm stand. A FoodCorps member leads elementary school students in gardening activities up the hill in the community garden plots that are managed by Cultivating Community.

The Grow Cart is a culmination of many of Cultivating Community's food access programs. Cultivating Community helps to coordinate the Maine Senior Farm Share program, connecting farmers with qualifying seniors. The senior share program provides low-income seniors with fifty-dollar credits to use at participating farm stands, thanks to a grant from the USDA. Seniors can sign up for the program through Cultivating Community, which then doubles the amount of produce in the recipients' share. Participating farmers simply drop produce off with Cultivating Community, leaving the coordination of the program to the nonprofit.[237]

The youth growers work to package the shares, adding their own produce from the Boyd Street Urban Farm and delivering shares to seniors. Aquilina sees participants making valuable connections through her organization's programs. "It's an important component for the youth to see where their food goes, for the youth to connect with seniors, for the seniors to connect with youth and for everyone to have fresh produce," she says. The Grow Cart will help expand this program with the delivery of senior and CSA shares. People will be able to buy produce at the mobile farm using their WIC and SNAP (food stamps) benefits.

Cultivating Community currently runs seven farm stands in the Portland area that occur weekly in the summer months, being set up outside schools, community centers, public housing sites and Whole Foods Market. These farm stands' vendors are all graduates of the New American Sustainable Agriculture Project (NASAP), a Cultivating Community program that trains immigrant and refugee farmers. The NASAP farmers are from South Sudan, Guatemala, Somalia and Mexico.[238]

NASAP provides farm skills training in Portland and on Cultivating Community's farm in Lisbon, thirty miles north of Portland. After graduating from the program, participating farmers run their own farm stand with a Cultivating Community staff member, who helps with customer service. "The goal is that after a year or two of that very structured one-on-one support, that farmer will be ready for a market independently," says Aquilina. "[They] will be ready to go to a farmers' market without someone there to smooth over transactions or provide assistance when necessary."[239]

Habiba Noor farms in Lisbon as part of Cultivating Community's New American Sustainable Agriculture Project. *Photo by Greta Rybus.*

The small farm stands are helping to create markets for new farmers, something Aquilina says is becoming increasingly needed. "After a while, there's this question of, 'There's so many farms; where are the markets?'" she says. "We're doing our best to increase market access, and then it's a matter of increasing the demand." To that end, Aquilina is working with Portland Public Schools Food Service director Ron Adams to increase local produce in school meals.[240]

Despite any challenges, Aquilina is encouraged by the intangible benefits of her programs, seen between the new farmers and their customers. "We have farmers who are at these farm stands, who are having direct interactions with other people in the community. That's creating a connection between people of different cultures and bringing them together over food," she says.[241] It's these connections that inspire Aquilina in her work to find more ways to bring local produce to the city's residents.

The Veggie Bus

Farmer Penny Jordan found a creative way to deliver her farm's fresh produce to those in need: a repurposed school bus. Jordan's Farm participates in the Maine Senior Farm Share program, serving 350 seniors a season. The traveling farm stand, dubbed the "Veggie Bus," delivers produce shares to program participants.[242]

Jordan remembers her brother's idea to convert an old school bus: "He came in one day and said, 'What do you think about a veggie bus?' I said, 'I think it's a great idea; when are we going to do it?'" The Jordans purchased a decommissioned school bus from the Cape Elizabeth school system. "He was so excited," she laughs.[243]

With the help of students from the Cape Elizabeth High School community service project and one of the farm's employees, the bus was transformed into a traveling farm stand. Jordan saw the need for the bus after seeing seniors struggling to visit the farm to redeem their farm shares. "It goes to senior housing sites because we had a gap [in] Senior Farm Share. We have 350 seniors who participate, and some of them don't have transportation." Now the bus serves seniors at their housing sites and the employees of several Greater Portland business parks.[244]

As a farmer, Jordan is well positioned to help address the gap between food production and access. She encourages her CSA customers to donate their remaining balances at the end of the season to purchase produce for food pantries.[245] Delivering produce in the Veggie Bus helps to increase her sales, of course, but also provides fresh produce to seniors in need.

Jordan sees her work addressing food insecurity as more than an obligation. "What's important to me is knowing that when I leave this earth, I have made a difference," she says. "I am a firm believer that we're all here to do something, and I really want what I do to have impacted wherever I am in some way."[246]

Salvaged Opportunities

Wayside Food Programs' Don Morrison has a challenge that he's trying to turn into an opportunity. It's seven o'clock on a Friday night, and a trucker has just called him, offering a pallet of frozen eggplant parmigiana dinner entrées. The trucker is en route to Walmart's distribution center in Lewiston and already knows that one pallet of his truckload will be rejected. As the man in charge of procuring food donations for his food rescue organization, Morrison is happy to accept the food. The problem is that one pallet of frozen dinner entrées is nine hundred pounds of food. The trucker has already called three food pantries, all of which were interested in just a few cases. But no one is able to handle the donation in its entirety.[247]

Morrison is faced with opportunities like this every day at Wayside Food Programs. He is happy to meet the trucker early on a Saturday morning to receive donations that would otherwise be thrown away. He has called the food pantries that he knows will come to take several cases for their organizations and the ones that he knows have the freezer capacity. He regularly meets deliveries like this one on weekends, late at night or early in the morning. "We know who to call, who will come quickly, and I know who will use how much. You really have to be connected and have your finger on the pulse of what everybody's doing. It's a challenge," Morrison says.[248]

Wayside Food Programs is unique in its ability to act as a distributor of rescued food to smaller food pantries. Located in an industrial neighborhood of Portland, Wayside has a large warehouse with two loading docks and a commercial kitchen. With walk-in coolers, freezers and lots of storage space, Wayside can handle large amounts of fresh and nonperishable food donations. Volunteers in the warehouse sort and store food donations into shelving units where staff from food pantries can come in and shop. Wayside serves forty-seven food agencies, two of which are its own mobile food pantry and community meals program.[249]

In the past few years, Morrison has had to get creative with his sources for rescued food. Wayside receives donations from grocery stores, hospitals, food manufacturers and distributors, trucking companies, farms and dairy processors. But as companies work to decrease their waste due to economic uncertainty and an increased interest in corporate environmental sustainability, food donations have decreased. At the same time, the recent economic recession has created an increased need for food pantry services.

Morrison cites the 2011 sale of Portland-based food manufacturer Barber Foods as an example. The company was purchased by an Ohio-based food manufacturing company that then upgraded the factory's equipment to help reduce waste.[250] Barber Foods donates its imperfect products to Wayside Food Programs, but with the new equipment, there was less waste and therefore fewer donations. In addition, the newer equipment required fewer workers to operate, resulting in the layoffs of about eighty people. Morrison says that this is but one example where decreasing food donations are coupled with an increasing demand for food pantry services.

Recently, Morrison attended the Crystal Lake Ice Fishing Derby, a sport ice fishing event that raises money for various charities and helps to control native and invasive species in the lake. Participants may keep the fish they catch, but this year, they were also able to donate their catch to Wayside Food Programs. The fish was filleted by seafood purveyor Salt + Sea, which frequently partners with Wayside Food Programs. The fish derby donation is part of a larger effort of the Maine Hunters for the Hungry program, which helps hunters donate their kill or a portion to food rescue organizations.[251]

The University of Maine Cooperative Extension's Maine Harvest for Hunger program is another growing source for Wayside's produce donations. Participating volunteers plant community garden plots or extra rows in their personal gardens and donate the extra produce to help alleviate hunger in Cumberland County. To date, 21,392 pounds of produce have been donated through the Maine Harvest for Hunger program.[252]

Through a network of trained volunteers, UMaine Extension has developed a number of garden sites that donate produce to the program. Its Master Gardener program trains volunteers with an extensive classroom learning program and then requires an annual volunteer commitment. Master Gardener volunteers then turn to volunteer projects like creating and maintaining gardens at food pantries and community gardens, in particular to grow produce for the Harvest for Hunger program.

UMaine Extension horticulturalist and program coordinator Amy Witt has seen an increasing number of participating gardens in the program.

Gardeners frequently dedicate a community garden plot to raising produce for the Maine Harvest for the Hungry program. *Photo by Greta Rybus.*

Originally a part of the national program Plant a Row for the Hungry, Witt and her co-workers began the Maine Harvest for Hunger program in 2011. Master Gardener volunteers and UMaine Extension staff built a garden at their offices at Tidewater Farm in Falmouth, just north of Portland. The 180-square-foot raised beds produced six hundred pounds of onions, beans, peppers, corn and greens for Wayside's food programs.[253]

Witt says that a statewide committee is looking at how to effectively use even more donated produce in food pantries. In particular, the committee is looking at how to extend the usefulness of these perishable produce donations. Produce donations can be extended by freezing or turning them into a value-added product, like tomato sauce.[254]

Food processing is particularly useful after volunteers glean unwanted produce from farms like Jordan's Farm and Maxwell's strawberry fields. While gleaning captures hundreds of pounds of produce that would otherwise be wasted, the practice also generates large volumes of perishable products all at once. Using volunteers to process produce, thus extending its shelf life, would help food pantries use more local products year round.

Witt loves working with Wayside's Don Morrison, as he picks up the Harvest for Hunger produce at garden sites and provides bins for gleaning.[255] Morrison excels at creating and streamlining the systems that make food rescue possible. More and more, Morrison is turning to these unique sources for salvaged food to meet the growing demand.

Although the numbers of people attending the food pantries are growing, Morrison knows that there's enough food out there to adequately feed them. "We have all these hungry people, and there's no shortage of food in this country. There's no shortage. We have a distribution problem," Morrison says.[256] With 1.7 million pounds of food rescued last year and thirty thousand community meals served, Morrison and his co-workers are certainly doing their part to solve that problem.[257]

Chapter 19

SWEET ENDINGS

L ike the city's restaurants, food businesses in Portland are frequently staffed by the owners. Walk into Dean's Sweets, the small chocolate shop on Middle Street, and you'll be greeted by owner Kristin Thalheimer, who jokingly refers to herself as "Dean's sweetie." Kristin will help you decide between milk and dark chocolate (answer: dark) and package up a delicate box of truffles for you. Her husband and business partner, Dean Bingham, is in the back of the shop, quietly at work making their products.

The couple opened a retail shop in 2008 after the production, packaging and shipping work of their truffle business outgrew their home. Bingham had been making truffles for years but didn't decide to make a business of it until he consulted Thalheimer as a business coach. Looking for a career change after years of architecture, Bingham considered making ice cream or chocolate. Talented at producing both, he ultimately decided on truffles because of their shelf stability and portability.

Thalheimer summarizes the motivation behind Dean's Sweets' genesis as equal parts entrepreneurial spirit and bleak economic outlook: "It seems like a trend in Maine that if you want to have a job, you have to create it yourself."[258] The two are well suited for that after years of being their own bosses working in the client-based service industry.

The first Dean's Sweets truffle sales happened at a contra dance festival in 2004, where Thalheimer remembers, "We sold them for some ridiculously low price. We put them in little plastic, round deli cups. And people gave us money for it, and we gave them chocolate, and a business was born."[259]

Dean Bingham and Kristin Thalheimer in their Old Port chocolate truffle shop, Dean's Sweets. *Photo by Kate McCarty.*

Thalheimer and Bingham slowly expanded the chocolate business, working from home while continuing with their respective day jobs. They now staff the shop full time but still maintain their business coaching and architecture consulting businesses.

Their Middle Street shop serves as both retail outlet and production space. Bingham heats cream for the truffles' fillings in an electric double boiler and melts chocolate on an induction burner. His first truffle flavors were the classics brandy and rum. Today, he makes upward of thirty flavors using local ingredients like chèvre and sea salt.

Bingham has few secrets about chocolate making, pointing out that the recipes can easily be found online. Rather, his flavor combinations and skilled hand make his truffles unique. Bingham makes a truffled version of a Needham, a traditional Maine candy made with mashed potatoes, coconut and confectioners sugar. The candies are named after either a Maine reverend who brought candies to church in the 1800s to entice people to attend or because people say, "Once you have 'em, you need 'em!" In lieu of mashed potatoes, Bingham flavors his Needham truffle filling with Maine's Cold River potato vodka and shredded coconut.

The whoopie pie, the official Maine state treat, is rumored to have been named because men would shout "Whoopie!" when they found the cakes in their lunchboxes. *Photo by Greta Rybus.*

Bingham's most unique flavor is a Moxie truffle. Moxie is a local soda invented in the 1900s by a Maine doctor looking for an energy tonic that didn't involve cocaine or alcohol.[260] The result was a drink similar to root beer but a bit bitter and medicinal. The soda was bought by Coca-Cola in 2007, and ardent Moxie fans say that it hasn't been the same since. Fortunately, Bingham's Moxie truffle doesn't taste too much like its namesake, but it makes "Moxie freaks" happy.

People draw parallels between Bingham's work as an architect and his chocolatier work. Bingham is certainly skilled at constructive processes that require attention to detail. Bingham was recognized by the American Institute of Architects for his design of the historic renovation of Portland's Grace Restaurant. The design of the church turned restaurant preserves many elements of the original building, like stained-glass windows, pews and the organ pipes integrated into the open kitchen's ventilation system.

But lately, Bingham says that he finds working with chocolate more rewarding. "Unlike architecture, where you do a project for someone and wait five years for a response…chocolate is instantaneous. Nine times out of ten, you get a wonderful response, which is very reassuring, uplifting and gratifying. The other business is painfully slow," he says.[261]

Both Bingham and Thalheimer seem happy to be a part of Portland's vibrant food industry. Thalheimer says, "Portland's been really welcoming to a small food business. I think our experience would have been really different had we tried to do this in Boston or even a suburb of Boston."[262] Instead, the two have found the perfect spot for their business on Middle Street's "foodie row," flanked by Eventide Oyster Co. and the Pepperclub.

Thalheimer complains that there's too much chocolate left in her house after the holidays. She says that she's been overdosing on M&Ms and laughs when I express my shock that the owner of a truffle shop eats Mars chocolate. Apparently, after making chocolate for almost a decade, the two aren't sick of it yet. "It's rare that I can't eat what I make," smiles Bingham.[263]

Finding Community in Baking

Alysia Zoidis is one Mainer who left the state for the big city, thinking that she'd never move back. But ten years later, she's the owner of East End Cupcakes, a successful bakery in Portland. Zoidis graduated from college in Boston with a degree in retail management and was working as a fashion merchandiser in New York City. She loved her career in the fashion industry and her job that kept her busy traveling around the country.

But her trips back to Maine to visit her family began to have a surprising effect on her: she found it harder and harder to leave. Zoidis started to see Portland through her parents' eyes, updating the vision of Maine left over from her suburban childhood. Their community was made up of artists, small business owners and chefs. This strong sense of community, she says, was completely lacking for her in New York. So she began plotting her move back to Portland.

Zoidis sits in her bright, airy Old Port shop, the dark exposed wooden beams offset by pale pink and gray accents, remembering the idea that launched her business. "Considering that I lived in New York and was surrounded by cupcake shops, I thought it took me a little too long to figure it out," she laughs. "I was like, 'Well, I could do a cookie bar'...and I'm standing in front of a cupcake shop."[264]

She had always been drawn to baking and fondly remembers baking with her family growing up, in particular with her grandmothers. Once she decided to launch a cupcake bakery in Portland, she was determined. When her mom suggested maybe having a back-up plan, Zoidis responded, "Nope. No back-up plan. This is the plan."

Zoidis moved to Portland and baked cupcakes in her apartment for one year while she continued to work and travel for her New York employer

Alysia Zoidis of East End Cupcakes in her Old Port shop. *Photo by Kate McCarty.*

remotely. She grew her business slowly, until a well-timed mention in *Maine* magazine garnered her more attention. After outgrowing her East End apartment kitchen, she opened her retail shop in July 2011. The Food Network's *Cupcake Wars* called shortly thereafter and asked her to compete.

Four years after leaving New York, Zoidis has baked hundreds of thousands of cupcakes and is part of a community of passionate food professionals. She prides herself on supporting local artists and craftsmen in the construction of her Fore Street retail shop. Her love for fashion and knack for artfully arranging spaces is apparent in the design of her bakery's space.

Zoidis regularly bakes vanilla, chocolate, red velvet and chocolate salted caramel cupcakes, as well as specialty flavors like chocolate with peanut butter and coconut with cream cheese. "I was looking for a creative outlet…and with cupcakes, there's always something you can do to be more creative. I was trying to take flavors I liked in real life and apply them to cupcake flavors, like the maple bacon and the pear and honey." The endless combinations of cakes and icing that Zoidis has created are a testament to the versatility of her chosen profession.

The winter afternoon I visit Zoidis in her shop is a relatively quiet one, frequented by a few customers and deliverymen. A construction worker from the new hotel across the street comes in for coffee. Zoidis rings him up at the counter and returns to the table and our conversation. After the man fills his coffee cup, he disappears into the back of her shop, causing Zoidis to pause midsentence. She laughs when she realizes that he's returning the creamer to the walk-in refrigerator. "Those are my customers; they're just right at home," she says.

It seems as though Zoidis has found the community she was missing in New York. Despite at times missing the creative energy of a bigger city, she says that she loves the quality of her life in Portland: "In the summer, when I get out early enough, I can be at the beach in twenty minutes. And I think, 'I was at work making cupcakes, and now I'm on the beach—this is so awesome!'"[265]

Neighborhood Bakery

Despite the years' worth of accolades and legions of dedicated customers, Standard Baking Co.'s Alison Pray insists that her bakery remain a neighborhood business, ensuring the freshest possible baked goods. "The whole point is to be local and neighborhood," she says. "If we need to go further than Brunswick, I feel like we should bake the bread there. Otherwise, we're just not a neighborhood bakery. It's about a twenty-minute drive, and that's as far as we'll go."[266]

To ensure that their breads and pastries are available fresh to their customers, the staff of Standard Baking Co. bake daily, the amounts informed by carefully collected data. Pray and her husband, Matt James, track sales using past years to inform their daily amounts. Because none of their products are held for sale the next day, Pray and James are looking to bake just enough for their steady stream of customers without any excess.

But ultimately, says James, "It's not a science."[267] Any number of changing factors contribute to how much bread they sell on any given day, especially in the winter. A snowstorm is particularly disruptive, although in Portland, a fair number of locals still make it out during storms for their daily bread ritual. Not so at the bakery's first location on Wharf Street, Pray remembers. The pedestrian-only street made it particularly difficult to operate a retail shop. When it snowed, says Pray, "nobody could get down Wharf Street. And we'd end up having to throw away an entire day's worth of work. In

The pastry case at Standard Baking Co. is full of buttery, sweet treats. *Photo by Kate McCarty.*

terms of a retail food business where you're making everything by hand, it was heartbreaking."[268]

Pray and James started Standard Baking Co. in 1996 after being inspired by the *boulangeries* and *patisseries* they frequented on a trip to France. The two were working at Street & Co. at the time and decided to bring a traditional European bakery to Portland. They moved to Boston to train at Clear Flour Bread in Brookline, an artisanal bakery that makes Italian, French and German breads and pastries. Upon their return to Portland in 1996, they opened a shop next to Street & Co. to bake baguettes and sell wholesale to the restaurant.

But after the first night their bread was served in the restaurant, retail customers came knocking. Rather, they walked right in to the small bakery early the next morning, asking for fresh baguettes. Pray and James remember their first two retail customers, a French man and woman who came in within hours of each other. "Both of them had been living in the U.S....for a long time, and they missed their daily bread ritual," says Pray. "And they both would come in every single day and still do."[269]

The two hung up a carved wooden baguette and began using an old cookie tin as a cash register. Eighteen years later, their operating systems aren't much more complex than that. The cookie tin has been upgraded to an actual cash register and an Excel spreadsheet to track sales. Many of the systems and pieces of equipment now used at Standard Baking Co. are the same as those at Clear Flour Bread, like the Belgian linen *couche* used to shape baguette dough and the German *brotform* baskets in which the country boules rise.

The store's branding consists of not much more than the bakery's name painted in black and white on the brick exterior of their building and a placeholder website. A friend once observed that the better a business's food, the worse its marketing and branding, and that seems to be the case with Standard Baking Co. It is immensely successful with word-of-mouth marketing alone, because its flaky croissants, crusty breads and buttery pastries speak for themselves.

Pray and James would probably disagree, looking at each other a little sheepishly when discussing their lack of marketing. Instead, the two are busy overseeing the daily operations of their business. Pray laughs when she finds herself detailing the ideal appearance of a baguette while eyeing a batch fresh from the oven. "I feel like I've been doing anything but baking for so long," she says.[270]

But that doesn't mean that Pray can't still discuss the intricacies of baking, pointing out the "ears" of a baguette, created by the traditional scoring of the dough. She details the different grain flours used for their breads and their work testing new Maine-grown wheat varietals from a new gristmill in Skowhegan. While showing me their massive custom-built Fringand oven, Pray alludes to her huge amounts of knowledge, saying, "Trying to master just how much steam you're going to let into the oven takes a long time. And you have to work through all seasons, all year round, multiple years, to really get a handle on it."[271]

The various conditions that can occur within the bakery and their ingredients, Pray explains, make the process of producing their quality breads different every day. Bakers and mixers are constantly adjusting for the weather, the seasons, varying moisture levels in the flour and the quality of the resulting dough. As Pray points out all the variables in the process, from mixing to baking, I marvel that her staff is able to turn out a consistently good product under such changing conditions.

Pray concedes that it can take years to master the skills of baking. After eighteen years of it, Pray herself is still learning. "We trained on the job," she says, "and there's a lot of continuing education. We're always going to classes and workshops and learning with other bakers. It seems endless, but that's what keeps it interesting. It is endless actually."[272]

It's these environmental variables that make each bakery unique. Nowhere is this more literally expressed than in Standard Baking Co.'s sourdough

Baguettes fresh out of the oven at Standard Baking Co. *Photo by Kate McCarty.*

starters. The starter, a bucketful of bubbling, organic white flour and water, is eighteen years old and contains "some real Portland flora," laughs Pray.[273] The constant feeding of the starter has made it seem like another member of the bakery staff. After learning that the bakery was broken into two years ago, one of the first questions the staff asked was if the sourdough starters were okay.

Their Francese bread, a mild sourdough, is served at Fore Street restaurant, which occupies the second floor of the bakery's building. The crusty bread is a perennial favorite at the restaurant, perfect for dipping in fruity olive oil before your meal or for soaking up the broth that accompanies the steamed mussels. The bread order is baked in the afternoon and then a server simply comes downstairs before dinner service to pick it up. Surely the fact that their bread is served at Fore Street and Street & Co., two of Portland's oldest and finest restaurants, contributes to Standard Baking Co.'s success.

After eighteen years of operation, Standard Baking Co. exists much as it did when it began. It has expanded its wholesale and retail operations, moved to a larger space and produces more, using bigger equipment, than when it started. But its dedication to its customers, to Portland and to quality ingredients is unwavering.

The stories of independent businesses like Dean's Sweets, East End Cupcakes and Standard Baking Co. are varied, but the owners all are united in their love for Portland and their dedication to the local economy. These businesses do more for the community than provide sweets to enamored tourists; they provide an antidote to the cultural homogenization of many American cities. Portland's sense of character is what attracts so many people to live, work and play in the city. The tasty treats available at these local businesses are just icing on the "buy local" cake.

Chapter 20

RIDING COFFEE'S THIRD WAVE

Outside, it was very dark, very cold and the city had just seen two back-to-back snowstorms, resulting in more than two feet of snow. But inside a small coffee shop on a December night, twenty people gathered to taste some French wine, sample a few snacks and talk. The red holiday lights gave the room a rosy glow, and the espresso machine caused the windows to steam over. Our host, Rosemont Market's Joe Appel, clinked his wine glass with a fork to interrupt the din of conversation. He thanked us all for coming out for a wine tasting on such a cold night and then reprised a conversation I'd had with him just minutes before.

The connections formed through events like this Rosemont Market and Tandem Coffee pairing are intangible, Appel says. The market and the coffee shop serve as places where you can eat and drink, satisfying your basic needs. But both businesses do more for the people they serve by creating community. Appel points out that Tandem Coffee doesn't even have a WiFi connection.[274] The Tandem Coffee shop is small, with only a few stools around the pour-over bar. There are no overstuffed chairs to occupy for hours while immersed in one's laptop. Drip coffee is made to order in the shop, encouraging a slower pace than you might otherwise find in a coffee shop. Customers end up lingering and talking with one another.

"It's like a little family down here," Tandem owner Kathleen Pratt said to me that morning.[275] She invited me to the evening's wine tasting, and that's how I found myself learning about the wines of Roussillon, France. I already felt like I was a part of the Tandem family.

Pratt feels strongly about making coffee accessible to her customers. She recalls how she felt moving to Portland to open a coffee shop: "We were nervous; we're out-of-towners coming from New York City and Blue Bottle [Coffee]. With that sort of résumé, maybe people thought we were going to be snobby and elitist. But I just want people to feel like they're walking into our home. We're here to help educate or talk to people and create a community."[276]

Kathleen and Will Pratt met in San Francisco while working for Blue Bottle Coffee. Will learned to roast coffee beans, while Kathleen managed Blue Bottle's Mint Plaza store and eventually oversaw the company's expansion to Brooklyn. Looking for a new place to move to, Will and Kathleen explored Portland by tandem bicycle one weekend and relocated shortly thereafter. They found the perfect space for their own coffee shop not one month later in an old warehouse in East Bayside.

The Pratts were surprised to find such a vibrant coffee scene, but they were thrilled to be part of a community that clearly loves its coffee. "Coffee is getting a lot of attention, and we're just lucky to be here at the right time," says Kathleen. Tandem Coffee joins the ranks of Coffee by Design, Bard, Speckled Ax and Arabica, all of which roast their own coffee. Kathleen was pleasantly surprised by Portland's individualized approach to serving coffee: "I'm used to there being a couple of roasters and then a bunch of different cafés serving those roasters as wholesale accounts. But here, all the main cafés are roasting their own, which is really unique."[277]

Will's approach to roasting coffee defines Tandem's signature style. Their coffees are a lighter roast, which is a popular trend in coffee roasting nationwide. Will and Kathleen buy their green coffee beans from a variety of importers, who source coffee from the "bean belt," in places like Ethiopia, Rwanda, Kenya, Mexico and Indonesia.

Will roasts coffee in the back of the shop, using a vintage twelve-kilo Probat drum roaster. Surrounded by burlap bags full of green coffee, Will monitors the beans being tossed around inside the roaster's drum. The coffee is packaged in half-pound bags marked with their signature tandem bicycle logo and labeled with tasting notes like grapefruit, vanilla, toffee and "Tootsie Roll finish."

A small one-pound sample roaster used for tastings sits on a table next to the larger roaster. Tandem employee and Blue Bottle Coffee alum Vien Dobui holds weekly cuppings or coffee tastings to teach customers about the different flavors of coffee. Dobui is also in charge of their wholesale accounts and training employees of restaurants that serve their coffee.[278]

Tandem can be found at Duckfat, where Chef Rob Evans has high praise for the small roastery: "I look at Tandem as some of the best coffee in the

Will Pratt of Tandem Coffee Roasters roasting coffee in his East Bayside coffee shop. *Photo by Kate McCarty.*

country. Especially since people say Blue Bottle is, and it's good coffee, but now they're a big business. Now Tandem is doing that small, craft thing right here in Portland."[279]

Tandem Coffee fits right into Portland's coffee community as part of the "third wave" of coffee in the United States. The first wave of coffee was the blended, often freeze-dried coffees that first brought widespread use of coffee into American households. The second wave of coffee then represents the specialty coffee movement, with espresso drinks and roasting operations. This is the coffee culture that most of us are familiar with now, thanks to second-wave company Starbucks. The third wave of coffee is a distillation of the second wave. Coffee roasters are now examining every step of coffee processing, from growing to harvesting to roasting to brewing.[280]

Tandem Coffee is the newest roastery in Portland embracing third-wave techniques, and Coffee by Design is the oldest. That does not mean, however, that CBD, as it's known around town, is stuck in the past. Rather than adopt every coffee brewing trend throughout their business's nineteen years, Coffee by Design owners Mary Allen Lindermann and Alan Spear carefully consider their company's every move. Lindermann and Spear are looking to uphold their core values of ensuring accessible, affordable specialty coffee for everyone.

Coffee by Design started in 1994 after Lindermann and Spear returned to Maine after ten years in Seattle. The couple wanted to bring the coffee culture of the West Coast to Portland and settled on an unlikely spot in what is now Portland's Arts District. In the early '90s, the area was known more for its porn theaters than art galleries. Despite an occupancy rate of 40 percent, small businesses like restaurants and artist-owned shops were opening on this part of Congress Street. Lindermann and Spear were looking to create a community space, and the up-and-coming neighborhood was the perfect spot for their vision.

Today, Coffee by Design has four coffeehouses in Portland and one in Freeport's L.L. Bean store. The business now employs more than forty-five people and just expanded to a new retail location. Its largest coffee shop yet, the Diamond Street location in Portland's East Bayside neighborhood, houses its roasting operation, offices and a retail coffee bar. The space includes room for training wholesale accounts' employees, offering educational events like cuppings and even a repair shop for brewing equipment. The coffee bar features equipment for several types of brewing methods, like Trifecta and Chemex brewers.

But despite the recent expansion, Coffee by Design has never been an exclusively profit-minded company. To that end, CBD has consciously chosen locations for its retail shops in areas of Portland that need economic and community development. Many have credited the original Congress Street location with revitalizing the neighborhood.[281] After its first location, Coffee by Design expanded to a Monument Square shop that was frequented by professionals on their way to and from the surrounding office buildings. Lindermann and Spear saw opportunity for growth through wholesale accounts into these offices but didn't feel that this direction was right for their company.[282]

Instead, they opened another retail shop on India Street and sold the Monument Square location. The India Street location was originally intended to house their new roasting operation with a retail store in the works. But the City of Portland encouraged Lindermann and Spear to open the retail shop at the same time as the roastery. After seeing the improvement their first coffee shop brought to its neighborhood, the city recognized that the India Street neighborhood would benefit from CBD's presence as well.

The India Street location is located next to a detoxification center, so Lindermann and Spear worked with the center's staff to see how the two businesses could coexist.[283] In the nine years since the India Street location has opened, Coffee by Design staff has succeeded in creating a community space for everyone who frequents the neighborhood shop.

With the opening of the Diamond Street location, Coffee by Design has certainly expanded, but with Lindermann and Spear's careful thought at every turn, it has done so in a way that continues to uphold their company's values. Lindermann and Spear have yet again found a space in a developing neighborhood for their newest shop. Their Diamond Street location is in a refurbished warehouse in East Bayside, a neighborhood that they had been considering for a location for ten years prior to their move. Originally zoned only for light manufacturing, many businesses in the area had to apply for rezoning to allow them to sell their products retail.

Lindermann has worked hard to continue accessibility and affordability of their coffee in their new coffee shop, despite what the advanced brewing methods might imply. She still believes in serving "specialty coffee without the attitude" by creating an environment where customers feel comfortable asking questions about her products. Lindermann and Spear put an incredible amount of thought and work into sourcing the best products for their businesses. They both travel to countries of origin and are familiar with the coffee farmers, some of whom they have been purchasing from for more than fifteen years.[284]

"It's almost as if we've just brought the customers along on the ride with us," says Lindermann. As she and her husband have traveled and learned about coffee, they've developed a sense of trust with their customers. Lindermann points to the time customers were asking for a certified Fair Trade version of Colombian coffee. Lindermann began selling a Fair Trade–certified Colombian coffee, but she found it to be of a lesser quality than the one she had been buying.

Despite the increased sales of the Fair Trade source's coffee, Lindermann decided to buy from her previous coffee supplier again. The farmer pays his workers more than minimum wage, offers pension plans and built schools and hospitals in his town, but his farm is too large to be certified Fair Trade. In switching to their original source, Lindermann and Spear realized that they had to communicate these decisions to their customers. "It's not about a sticker on a bag," says Lindermann. "It's about a relationship you develop."[285]

These relationships—between Lindermann and her coffee suppliers, between customers and baristas and between coffee roasters like Coffee by Design and Tandem Coffee—drive the evolution of Portland's coffee culture. Just as Starbucks' move into Portland in the mid-'90s boosted Coffee by Design's business, the deliberate growth of Coffee by Design has helped to foster a sophisticated coffee culture in Portland. And now there are as many options for a quality cup of joe as there are coffee drinkers seeking them out.

CONCLUSION

In researching this book, I met many of Portland's dedicated food professionals. I watched while they made cheese, planted spinach, roasted coffee beans and pickled vegetables. I talked with chefs before their restaurants opened, in the relative quiet of the kitchen. I followed farmers up and down the rows inside their greenhouses and talked over cups of tea with cream from the farmer's cow. I stepped in countless questionable puddles on the wharves while talking with mussel farmers, fishmongers and lobstermen. I cold-called some of the most well-regarded chefs in Portland and was greeted warmly every time.

Along the way, I witnessed firsthand the work of creative and passionate individuals who are attracted to the quality of life that our small city offers. I learned that affordable restaurant and retail space offers culinary professionals the opportunity to pursue food-based businesses in a supportive community. A population of enthusiastic diners bolstered by a seasonal tourist economy has created an unusually high-caliber culinary scene for a city of Portland's size.

Support for local foods is especially strong in Maine, as residents gravitate toward resilient and independent economies. A MOFGA opinion poll conducted in 2010 showed that the majority of Maine residents who purchase local foods do so to help support local farmers and to support the local economy.[286] Russell Libby, former executive director of MOFGA, wrote in the survey's summary, "These answers tell an important story. When the economy we have been relying on doesn't work, people turn to one another, to their communities. Farmers (and fishermen) are an important part of those local economies."[287]

To create an independent local food economy, farmers need to grow, raise or harvest enough food to feed Maine's 1.3 million residents.[288] MOFGA marketing consultant Cheryl Wixson assessed the state's agricultural output and created a list of twenty foods that Maine produces enough of for the state's residents to enjoy all year.[289]

The "Maine Twenty" encompasses lobster, blueberries and potatoes, of course, but also vegetables like beets, greens and tomatoes. Maine produces enough dairy products and meat to meet its citizens' consumption of these foods, as well as dried beans, honey and eggs. Local food system advocates can use the "Maine Twenty" to determine what foods can be sourced locally, as well as barriers to local food use.[290]

But in the discussion of economic independence and environmental sustainability, one important part of eating can be lost: the pleasure. Eating locally grown foods is the easiest choice when the food tastes good. Portland chefs have embraced the use of local foods to create a fun, creative and varied dining scene.

When I asked food blogger Anestes Fotiades about the significance of local foods in Portland restaurants, he responded:

> [T]*he greatest impact I see is* [the] *relationships that local food forges between farmers, fishermen, other food producers and restaurants. Those connections are what's created the environment that enabled the Maine restaurant scene to grow and thrive. They spur creativity and create a community of individuals that provide great dining experiences for locals and tourists alike. The Portland food scene would be a shadow of itself if it weren't for the access chefs have to local food.*[291]

Portland's access to fresh ingredients from nearby farms and the ocean has attracted a passionate population of cooks and diners. I'm lucky to have stumbled into a city with a dynamic food scene, where there's no shortage of opinions about restaurants, food and cooking. There's always room for improvement (like the cuisines that people perpetually complain are missing). The dining scene will continue to change, for better or for worse, depending on one's viewpoint. But it's an exciting time to dine in the culinary capital of Maine, as our vibrant food scene continues to produce enticing new options.

NOTES

Chapter 1

1. Portland, Maine City Planning, "WCZ Policy."
2. Krista Desjarlais, interview with the author, September 30, 2013.
3. Ibid.
4. Michael Quigg, interview with the author, July 25, 2013.
5. Sam Hayward, interview with the author, November 12, 2013.
6. Smith, "It Takes the Village," *The Bollard*.
7. Amato's, "Our History."
8. Krista Desjarlais, interview with the author, September 30, 2013.
9. Michael Quigg, e-mail to the author, July 29, 2013.
10. Sam Hayward, interview with the author, November 12, 2013.
11. Ibid.
12. Krista Desjarlais, interview with the author, September 30, 2013.
13. Rob Evans, interview with the author, December 18, 2013.

Chapter 2

14. Rob Evans, interview with the author, December 18, 2013.
15. Ibid.

16. Food & Wine website.

17. James Beard Foundation website.

18. Rob Evans, interview with the author, December 18, 2013.

19. Ibid.

20. Travel Channel, "Bizarre Foods Episodes."

21. Food & Wine website.

22. Rob Evans, interview with the author, December 18, 2013.

23. Ibid.

24. Arlin Smith, interview with the author, September 10, 2013.

25. Ibid.

26. Rob Evans, interview with the author, December 18, 2013.

Chapter 3

27. John Bliss, interview with the author, October 30, 2013.

28. Sam Hayward, interview with the author, November 12, 2013.

29. Damian Sansonetti, interview with the author, December 30, 2013.

30. Ibid.

31. Ibid.

32. Local 188 website.

33. Jay Villani, interview with the author, October 17, 2013.

34. Alison Pray, interview with the author, January 20, 2014.

35. Ibid.

36. Abby Huckel, interview with the author, January 21, 2014.

37. Kelly Rioux, interview with the author, January 21, 2014.

38. Ibid.

39. Will Garfield, interview with the author, December 19, 2013.

40. Emily Phillips, interview with the author, January 14, 2014.

41. Will Garfield, interview with the author, December 19, 2013.

42. Jason Williams, interview with the author, September 9, 2013.

43. The Well at Jordan's Farm website.

44. Jason Williams, interview with the author, September 9, 2013.

45. Ibid.

46. Ibid.

Chapter 4

47. Hemmerdinger, "Food-Service Transitions," *Portland Press Herald*.
48. Arlin Smith, interview with the author, September 10, 2013.
49. Ibid.
50. Ibid.
51. David Turin, interview with the author, November 7, 2013.
52. Ibid.
53. Ibid.
54. Will Garfield, interview with the author, December 19, 2013.
55. Ibid.
56. Ibid.
57. Ibid.
58. Ibid.
59. Ibid.
60. David Turin, interview with the author, November 7, 2013.

Chapter 5

61. Damian Sansonetti, interview with the author, December 30, 2013.
62. Ibid.
63. Rob Evans, interview with the author, December 18, 2013.
64. Damian Sansonetti, interview with the author, December 30, 2013.
65. Ibid.
66. David Turin, interview with the author, November 7, 2013.
67. Krista Desjarlais, interview with the author, September 30, 2013.
68. Goad, "Portland Restaurant Space Rare," *Portland Press Herald*.
69. Rob Evans, interview with the author, December 18, 2013.

Chapter 6

70. Penny Jordan, interview with the author, August 30, 2013.
71. Andrew Plant, discussion with the author, September 9, 2013.

72. Penny Jordan, interview with the author, August 30, 2013.
73. Ibid.
74. Cape Farm Alliance website.
75. Libby, "Why Local?," *Maine Organic Farmer & Gardener*.
76. Penny Jordan, interview with the author, August 30, 2013.
77. United States Census Bureau website.
78. National Conservation Easement Database website.
79. Mark Kerr, e-mail message to the author, September 30, 2013.
80. Penny Jordan, interview with the author, August 30, 2013.
81. Maine Organic Farmers & Gardeners Association website.
82. Green Spark Farm website.
83. Andrew Marshall, interview with the author, September 16, 2013.
84. Austin Chadd, interview with the author, October 24, 2013.
85. Broadturn Farm website.
86. John Bliss, interview with the author, October 20, 2013.
87. Ibid.
88. Maine Farmland Trust website.
89. John Bliss, interview with the author, October 20, 2013.

Chapter 7

90. Tyler Renaud, interview with the author, October 17, 2013.
91. Dorothee Grimm, interview with the author, October 2, 2013.
92. Ibid.
93. Silvery Moon Creamery website.
94. Pineland Farms website.
95. Eric Rector, e-mail to the author, October 22, 2013.
96. Ibid.
97. Dorothee Grimm, interview with the author, October 2, 2013.
98. Maine Cheese Guild website.
99. Maine Milk Commission website.
100. Bridgers, "Smiling Hill Farm Holding Its Own," Keep Me Current.
101. Sarah Wiederkehr, interview with the author, November 14, 2013.
102. Ibid.
103. Ibid.

104. Ibid.
105. Rosemont Market & Bakery website.
106. Sarah Wiederkehr, interview with the author, November 14, 2013.

Chapter 8

107. Davistown Museum, "Native American Special Topics."
108. Schmitt, "Maine Oyster Cult," *Maine Boats, Homes, and Harbors.*
109. Jacobsen, *Geography of Oysters*, 3.
110. Abigail Carroll, interview with the author, July 30, 2013.
111. Department of Maine Resources, "Aquaculture Lease Inventory."
112. Abigail Carroll, interview with the author, July 30, 2013.
113. Ibid.
114. Ibid.
115. Kathleen Taggersell, e-mail to the author, January 31, 2014.
116. Department of Marine Resources, "Blue Mussel."
117. Matt Moretti, interview with the author, August 27, 2013.
118. Ibid.
119. Ocean Approved website.
120. Bangs Island Mussels website.

Chapter 9

121. Department of Marine Resources website.
122. Brian Rapp, interview with the author, October 9, 2013.
123. Department of Marine Resources, "Historical Maine Fisheries Landings Data."
124. Dave Lalibertie, interview with the author, October 9, 2013.
125. Department of Marine Resources, "Guide to Lobstering in Maine."
126. Ibid.
127. B&M Beans website.
128. University of Maine Lobster Institute, "Lobstering Basics."

129. Ibid.

130. B&M Beans website.

131. Luzer, "How Lobster Got Fancy," *Pacific Standard.*

132. Alex Curtis, interview with the author, February 1, 2014.

133. Department of Marine Resources, "Historical Maine Fisheries Landings Data."

134. Alex Curtis, interview with the author, February 1, 2014.

135. New England Aquarium website.

136. Maine Lobster Marketing Collaborative website.

137. Bell, "So You Want to Be a Lobsterman," *Portland Press Herald.*

Chapter 10

138. Gulf of Maine Council on the Marine Environment, "Gulf of Maine in Context."

139. NOAA, "Brief History of Groundfishing Industry."

140. Ibid.

141. Gulf of Maine Research Institute, "Seafood Branding Program."

142. Hannaford, "Sustainable Seafood."

143. Jen Levin, interview with the author, January 10, 2014.

144. Ibid.

145. Ibid.

146. Gulf of Maine Research Institute, "Out of the Blue."

147. Charlie Bryon, interview with the author, January 11, 2014.

148. Jen Levin, interview with the author, January 10, 2014.

149. Ibid.

150. Ibid.

151. Damian Sansonetti, interview with the author, December 30, 2013.

152. Will Garfield, interview with the author, December 19, 2013.

153. Ibid.

154. Ibid.

155. Justine Simon, interview with the author, October 3, 2013.

156. Salt + Sea website.

157. Justine Simon, interview with the author, October 3, 2013.

158. Ibid.
159. Ibid.
160. Ibid.
161. Ibid.
162. Wayside Food Programs, "Justine Simon."

Chapter 11

163. Chris Miller, interview with the author, November 15, 2013.
164. Nick Branchina, interview with the author, January 16, 2014.
165. Ibid.
166. Browne Trading Company website.
167. Nick Branchina, interview with the author, January 16, 2014.
168. Rob Evans, interview with the author, December 18, 2013.
169. Portland, Maine City Planning, "WCZ Policy."
170. Goad, "Harbor Fish Market," *Portland Press Herald*.
171. Alfiero, *Harbor Fish Market*, 21.
172. Ibid.
173. Ibid., 27.
174. Ibid., 47.
175. Ibid., 34.

Chapter 12

176. Portland, Maine City website.
177. Portland Farmers' Market website.
178. Carolyn Snell, interview with the author, October 25, 2013.
179. Ibid.
180. Ibid.
181. Ibid.
182. Stephanie Aquilina, interview with the author, December 10, 2013.
183. Carolyn Snell, interview with the author, October 25, 2013.

Chapter 13

184. Rosemont Market & Bakery website.
185. Joe Appel, interview with the author, October 13, 2013.
186. Ibid.
187. Martha Putnam, interview with the author, January 14, 2014.
188. Joe Appel, interview with the author, October 13, 2013.
189. Maine Sustainable Agriculture Society website.
190. Martha Putnam, interview with the author, January 14, 2014.
191. Ibid.
192. Ibid.
193. Joe Appel, interview with the author, October 13, 2013.

Chapter 14

194. Kris Horton, interview with the author, November 7, 2013.
195. Bruner Foundation, "1999 Rudy Bruner Award."
196. Kris Horton, interview with the author, November 7, 2013.
197. Ibid.
198. Ibid.
199. Ibid.
200. Ibid.
201. Ibid.

Chapter 15

202. Town of Cape Elizabeth website.
203. Creative Portland website.
204. Sarah Sutton, interview with the author, November 25, 2013.
205. Ibid.
206. Ibid.
207. Karl Sutton, interview with the author, November 25, 2013.
208. Bill Leavy, interview with the author, October 23, 2013.

209. Ibid.
210. Karl Deuben, interview with the author, October 23, 2013.
211. Ibid.
212. Ibid.
213. Bill Leavy, interview with the author, October 23, 2013.
214. Sarah Sutton, interview with the author, November 25, 2013.
215. Karl Sutton, interview with the author, November 25, 2013.

Chapter 16

216. Katie Schier-Potocki, interview with the author, October 15, 2013.
217. Pocket Brunch website.
218. Nan'l Meiklejohn, interview with the author, October 15, 2013.
219. Brenner, "Meet Pocket Brunch," "Broadturn Farm" blog.
220. Nan'l Meiklejohn, interview with the author, October 15, 2013.
221. Katie Schier-Potocki, interview with the author, October 15, 2013.
222. Fotiades, "Under Construction," "Portland Food Map" blog.
223. Katie Schier-Potocki, interview with the author, October 15, 2013.

Chapter 17

224. Rachelle Curran Apse, interview with the author, January 15, 2014.
225. Ibid.
226. Ibid.
227. Ibid.
228. Abby Huckel, interview with the author, January 21, 2014.
229. Kelly Rioux, interview with the author, January 21, 2014.
230. Ibid.
231. Rachelle Curran Apse, interview with the author, January 15, 2014.

Chapter 18

232. Preble Street Resource Center website.

233. United States Census Bureau website.

234. Stephanie Aquilina, interview with the author, December 10, 2013.

235. Ibid.

236. Cultivating Community website.

237. Stephanie Aquilina, interview with the author, December 10, 2013.

238. Cultivating Community, *Beyond the Vegetable*, 27, 31, 39, 45.

239. Stephanie Aquilina, interview with the author, December 10, 2013.

240. Ibid.

241. Ibid.

242. Penny Jordan, interview with the author, August 30, 2013.

243. Ibid.

244. Ibid.

245. Jordan's Farm website.

246. Penny Jordan, interview with the author, August 30, 2013.

247. Don Morrison, interview with the author, January 28, 2014.

248. Ibid.

249. Ibid.

250. AdvancePierre, "AdvancePierre Foods Continues Growth."

251. Wayside Food Programs, "Hunters for the Hungry Program."

252. University of Maine Cooperative Extension, "Maine Harvest for Hunger."

253. Ibid., "Demonstration Garden at Tidewater Farm."

254. Amy Witt, interview with the author, February 7, 2014.

255. Ibid.

256. Don Morrison, interview with the author, January 28, 2014.

257. Ibid.

Chapter 19

258. Kristin Thalheimer, interview with the author, January 3, 2014.

259. Ibid.

260. Moxie website.

261. Dean Bingham, interview with the author, January 3, 2014.

262. Kristin Thalheimer, interview with the author, January 3, 2014.

263. Dean Bingham, interview with the author, January 3, 2014.

264. Alysia Zoidis, interview with the author, January 8, 2013.

265. Ibid.

266. Alison Pray, interview with the author, January 20, 2014.

267. Matt James, interview with the author, January 20, 2014.

268. Alison Pray, interview with the author, January 20, 2014.

269. Ibid.

270. Ibid.

271. Ibid.

272. Ibid.

273. Ibid.

Chapter 20

274. Joe Appel, discussion with the author, December 16, 2013.

275. Kathleen Pratt, interview with the author, December 16, 2013.

276. Ibid.

277. Ibid.

278. Ibid.

279. Rob Evans, interview with the author, December 18, 2013.

280. Skeie, "Norway and Coffee," *The Flamekeeper*.

281. Smith, "Quality Control," *Mainebiz*, 1.

282. Mary Allen Lindermann, interview with the author, January 27, 2014.

283. Ibid.

284. Ibid.

285. Ibid.

Conclusion

286. Libby, "Why Local?," *Maine Organic Farmer & Gardener*.

287. Ibid.

288. United States Census Bureau, "State & County Quick Facts."

289. Wixson, "Maine Local Twenty," *Maine Organic Farmer & Gardener*.

290. Ibid.

291. Anestes Fotiades, e-mail to the author, February 20, 2014.

BIBLIOGRAPHY

AdvancePierre Foods. "AdvancePierre Foods Continues Growth by Acquiring Barber Foods." June 1, 2011. www.advancepierre.com/Blog/News/Archives/2011/06/AdvancePierre-Foods-Continues-Growth-By-Acquiring-Barber-Foods.aspx.

Alfiero, Kathleen, Rian Alfiero and Nick Alfiero. *Harbor Fish Market: Seafood Recipes from Maine.* Rockport, ME: Down East Books, 2013.

Amato's. "Our History." www.amatos.com/our-history.

B&M Beans. "History." www.bmbeans.com/bm_history.asp.

Bangs Island Mussels. http://bangsislandmussels.com.

Bell, Tom. "So You Want to Be a Lobsterman." *Portland Press Herald,* August 14, 2011. www.pressherald.com/news/so-you-want-to-be-a-lobsterman_2011-08-14.html.

Brenner, Stacy. "Meet Pocket Brunch." "Broadturn Farm" blog, January 15, 2013. http://broadturnfarm.blogspot.com/2013/01/meet-pocket-brunch.html.

Bridgers, Leslie. "Smiling Hill Farm Holding Its Own, for Now." Keep Me Current, February 5, 2009. www.keepmecurrent.com/american_journal/news/smiling-hill-farm-holding-its-own-for-now/article_e57a8977-14b4-5854-b79c-fe5453b0f9c9.html.

Broadturn Farm. http://broadturnfarm.blogspot.com.

Browne Trading Company. "History of Browne Trading." www.brownetrading.com/about/history-of-browne-trading.

Bruner Foundation. "1999 Rudy Bruner Award: Portland Public Market." www.brunerfoundation.org/rba/pdfs/1999/02_Portland.pdf.

Cape Farm Alliance. http://capefarmalliance.org/about/history-mission-goals.

Creative Portland. http://liveworkportland.org.

Cultivating Community. *Beyond the Vegetable.* Portland, ME: self-published, 2013. Designed by Hannah Merchant.

———. "Mission." http://cultivatingcommunity.org/about/our-mission.html.

Davistown Museum. "Native American Special Topics." www.davistownmuseum.org/bibNorCont.htm#shellheaps.

Department of Marine Resources. "Aquaculture Lease Inventory." www.maine.gov/dmr/aquaculture/leaseinventory.

———. "Blue Mussel." www.maine.gov/dmr/rm/bluemussel.html.

———. "A Guide to Lobstering in Maine." www.maine.gov/dmr/rm/lobster/guide.

———. "Historical Maine Fisheries Landings Data." www.maine.gov/dmr/commercialfishing/historicaldata.htm.

Food & Wine. "Best New Chefs 2004." www.foodandwine.com/best_new_chefs/rob-evans.

Fotiades, Anestes. "Under Construction: The Jewel Box." "Portland Food Map" blog, January 7, 2014. www.portlandfoodmap.com/blognframe.html?/news/2014/01/07/under-construction-the-jewel-box.

Goad, Meredith. "Harbor Fish Market: A Whopper of a Story." *Portland Press Herald,* September 4, 2013. www.pressherald.com/life/foodanddining/fish-story_2013-09-04.html.

———. "Portland Restaurant Space Rare, Too Pricey, Chefs Say." *Portland Press Herald,* December 30, 2013. www.pressherald.com/news/Restaurant_space_rare_too_pricey__chefs_say.html.

Green Spark Farm. www.greensparkfarm.com.

Gulf of Maine Council on the Marine Environment. "The Gulf of Maine in Context." June 2010. www.gulfofmaine.org/state-of-the-gulf/docs/the-gulf-of-maine-in-context.pdf.

Gulf of Maine Research Institute. "Culinary Partners." www.gmri.org/culinarypartners.

———. "Out of the Blue." www.gmri.org/outoftheblue.

———. "Seafood Branding Program." www.gmri.org/community/display.asp?a=5&b=25&c=189.

Hannaford. "Sustainable Seafood." www.hannaford.com/content.jsp?pageName=SeafoodSustainability&leftNavArea=FoodLoveLeftNav.

Hemmerdinger, J. "Food-Service Transitions: Chain Restaurants on the Way In." *Portland Press Herald*, January 29, 2011. www.pressherald.com/news/on-the-way-in_2011-01-29.html.

Jacobsen, Rowen. *A Geography of Oysters: The Connoisseur's Guide to Oyster Eating in North America.* New York: Bloomsbury USA, 2007.

James Beard Foundation. "2009 JBF Award Winners." www.jamesbeard.org/awards?year[value][year]=2009&status=1&category=9879.

Jordan's Farm. "Help Prevent Hunger." www.jordansfarm.com/#!gallery/c1m3p.

Libby, Russell. "Why Local? Why Organic?" *The Maine Organic Farmer & Gardener* (Fall 2010). www.mofga.org/Publications/MaineOrganicFarmerGardener/Fall2010/LibbyEditorial/tabid/1736/Default.aspx.

Local 188. www.local188.com.

Luzer, Daniel. "How Lobster Got Fancy." *Pacific Standard*, June 7, 2013. www.psmag.com/navigation/business-economics/how-lobster-got-fancy-59440.

Maine Cheese Guild. www.mainecheeseguild.org.

Maine Farmland Trust. http://mainefarmlandtrust.org.

Maine Lobster Marketing Collaborative. www.lobsterfrommaine.com.

Maine Milk Commission. www.maine.gov/dacf/milkcommission/index.shtml.

Maine Organic Farmers and Gardeners Association. www.mofga.org.

Maine Sustainable Agriculture Society. http://mesas.org.

Moxie. "History." www.drinkmoxie.com/history.php.

National Conservation Easement Database. "Jordan Farm." http://www.conservationeasement.us/projects/135937.

New England Aquarium. "What Is the Impact of Warmer Waters on Lobsters?" http://www.neaq.org/conservation_and_research/climate_change/effects_on_ocean_animals.php#lobsters.

NOAA. "Brief History of the Groundfishing Industry of New England." www.nefsc.noaa.gov/history/stories/groundfish/grndfsh1.html.

Ocean Approved. www.oceanapproved.com.

Pineland Farms. www.pinelandfarms.org.

Pocket Brunch. http://pocketbrunch.com.

Portland Farmers' Market. "History." www.portlandmainefarmersmarket.org/history.htm.

Portland, Maine City Code. "Farmer's Markets." www.portlandmaine.gov/citycode/chapter021.pdf.

Portland, Maine City Planning. "WCZ Policy & Zoning Process." www.portlandmaine.gov/planning/wcz.asp.

Preble Street Resource Center. www.preblestreet.org.

Rosemont Market & Bakery. http://www.rosemontmarket.com.

Salt + Sea. http://saltandsea.me.

Schmitt, Catherine. "Maine Oyster Cult." *Maine Boats, Homes, and Harbors* (February/March 2008). Maine Sea Grant. www.seagrant.umaine.edu/files/pdf-global/08CSoystMBHH.pdf.

Silvery Moon Creamery. www.silverymooncheese.com.

Skeie, Trish. "Norway and Coffee." *The Flamekeeper* (Spring 2003). http://timwendelboe.no/uploads/the-flamekeeper-2003.pdf.

Smith, Peter. "It Takes the Village." *The Bollard*, July 31, 2006. http://thebollard.com/2006/07/31/it-takes-the-village.

Smith, Taylor. "Quality Control." *Mainebiz*, March 21, 2005.

Town of Cape Elizabeth. "Fort Williams Park." www.capeelizabeth.com/visitors/attractions/fort_williams_park/home.html.

Travel Channel. "Bizarre Foods Episodes & Travel Guides: Maine." www.travelchannel.com/tv-shows/bizarre-foods/episodes/maine-trip.

United States Census Bureau. "State & County Quick Facts." http://quickfacts.census.gov/qfd/states/23000.html.

University of Maine Cooperative Extension. "Demonstration Garden at Tidewater Farm." http://umaine.edu/cumberland/programs/garden.

———. "Maine Harvest for Hunger." http://umaine.edu/cumberland/programs/maine-harvest-for-hunger.

University of Maine Lobster Institute. "Lobstering Basics—History." http://umaine.edu/lobsterinstitute/education/lobstering-basics/history.

Wayside Food Programs. "Hunters for the Hungry Program Puts Food on Local Tables." www.waysidemaine.org/article/hunters-hungry-program-puts-food-local-tables.

———. "Justine Simon, Salt + Sea." www.waysidemaine.org/article/justine-simon-salt-sea.

The Well at Jordan's Farm. http://jordansfarm.wix.com/thewell.

Wixson, Cheryl. "Maine Local Twenty: More Maine Food on Maine Plates." *The Maine Organic Farmer & Gardener* (Spring 2010). www.mofga.org/Publications/MaineOrganicFarmerGardener/Spring2010/MaineLocalTwenty/tabid/1559/Default.aspx.

INDEX

ABOUT THE AUTHOR

Kate McCarty is a blogger and community educator from Monkton, Maryland. She has a degree in philosophy from St. Mary's College of Maryland and teaches food preservation at the University of Maine Cooperative Extension. She blogs about Maine food at "The Blueberry Files" (www.blueberryfiles.com) and writes a monthly food column for the *Portland Phoenix*. This is her first book. She lives in Portland, Maine, with her boyfriend and their two cats.

Photo by Greta Rybus.